Design

Towering pagodas and flight decks – of all the dreadnoughts in history, the *Fuso* and *Ise* class battleships are surely among the most curious.

Designed and built in an age when the big gun reigned supreme, the four ships could reasonably be described as experimental. Quickly left behind by the rapid pace of naval development, as early as 1920 there was no place for them in the Japanese Navy as efforts were concentrated on the 16in gunned ships of the *Nagato*, *Tosa*, *Amagi*, and *Kii* classes. If it were not for the Washington Treaty of 1922, which imposed a world-wide moratorium on new battleship construction thus forcing the cancellation of all but the *Nagato* class, the ships would probably have been scrapped in the 1930s, a fate met by many of their First World War contemporaries. As it was, the *Fuso* and *Ise* classes had no role in the Second World War until circumstances dictated their use in futile attempts to turn the tide of a war already lost. Nonetheless, they remain fascinating ships and, as with many of their contemporaries, their story begins in 1906 with the completion of HMS *Dreadnought*.

The appearance of the all-big-gun turbine-powered *Dreadnought* rendered all existing battleships obsolete overnight, and in response the rest of the world's navies initiated massive construction programs. Despite having the world's only battle-tested steel-built navy as a result of victory in the Russo-Japanese war, the Japanese Navy was forced to follow suit. Financially hobbled by the costs of that war, it took until 1909 for Japan's first dreadnoughts of the *Kawachi* class to be completed. By then the rest of the world's major navies had gained an insurmountable lead in the number of dreadnoughts in service or under construction. Recognising the futility of trying to compete in sheer numbers, the Japanese Navy adopted a quality before quantity approach, building fewer ships each of much greater capability than foreign designs.

In 1911 the Japanese government passed the Emergency Naval Expansion bill which authorised the building of four battlecruisers and one battleship. The battlecruisers were to be designed in Britain where the first of the class was to be built; these ships became the *Kongo* class. The battleship was to be designed and built in Japan; this ship became the *Fuso*.

There were a number of foreign designs to take into consideration when it came

Below: *Fuso* on trials, 24 August 1915, showing her clean lines as first built. Turret No 6 is not yet complete as evidenced by the large structure fitted aft in its place. The rangefinder can just be made out atop turret No 2 *(Author's collection)*

General arrangements of *Fuso* as completed, 1915. Note that the barbette of turret No 4 is higher than turret No 3. The location of the torpedo tubes can be seen below the waterline. *(Drawing by George Richardson)*

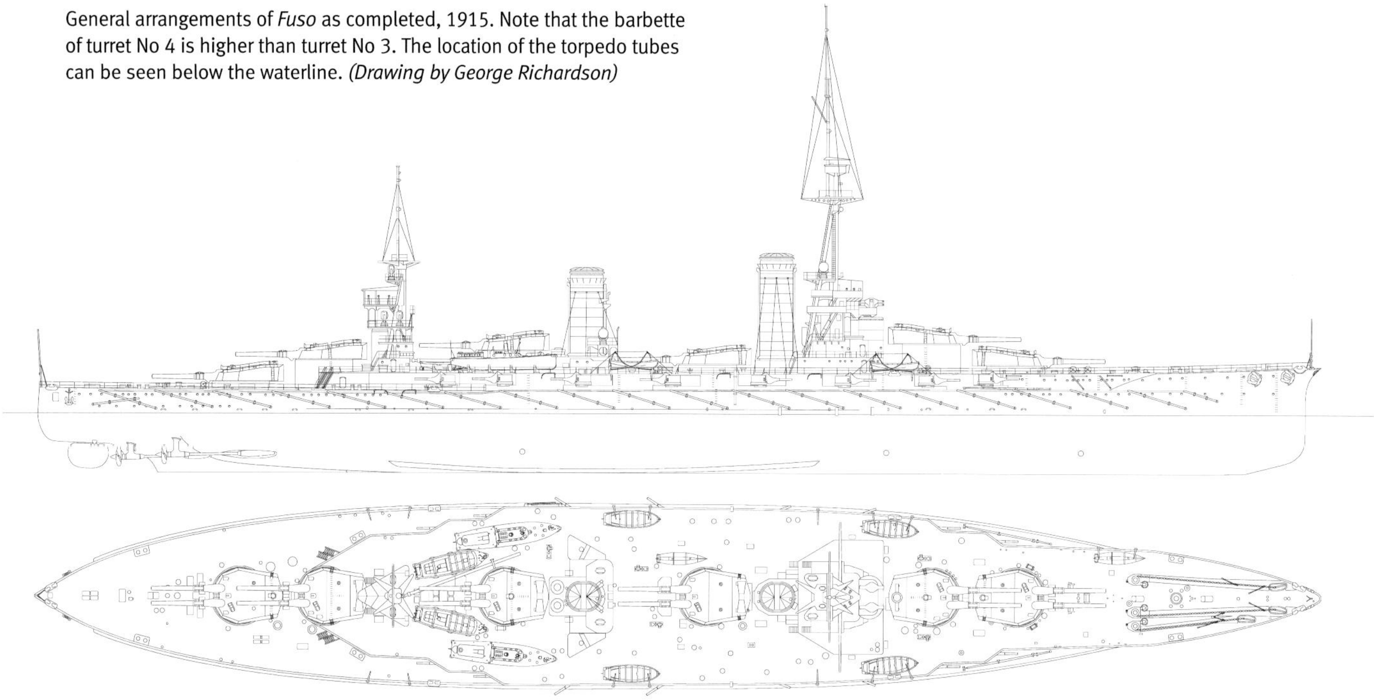

time to decide the main armament for the new ships. In Britain, the Royal Navy's new super-dreadnoughts of the *Orion* class were armed with the 13.5in gun. The US was building the *Wyoming* class with 12–12in guns and the succeeding *New York* class would be armed with 10–14in weapons. It was decided to leap over the competition and fit the new ships with the 14in gun then under development in Britain. To establish gunfire superiority over the *Orion*, *Wyoming*, and *New York* classes, *Fuso* would carry 12–14in.

The Japanese technical team working on the *Kongo* had access to both twin and triple turret designs for the 14in gun and many studies were carried out to decide the optimal layout of guns and turrets. The layout of six twin turrets eventually chosen was considered defensively superior as the loss of one turret would reduce the available firepower by only two guns. It was also felt that more gun turrets meant that more targets could be engaged simultaneously. Two turrets were fitted forward, two aft, and two amidships fore and aft of the second funnel.

Armament was not the only area where the battleship was intended to be superior to foreign designs; it was also to be at least 2 knots faster. The powerful machinery required to obtain the higher speed coupled with fitting six turrets required a longer hull than foreign designs, which in turn meant more space to be protected by armour plate.

NAMES

Ship	Meaning of Name	Pronounciation
Fuso	One of the ancient names for Japan	Who-So
Yamashiro	Ancient province on Honshu	Ya-ma-sheer-o
Ise	Ancient province on Honshu	E-Say
Hyuga	Ancient province on Kyushu	Hew-ga

The trade-offs between speed, protection, and firepower meant that *Fuso* would be much larger than her foreign contemporaries, but not as well protected. *Fuso* would end up 110ft longer than the *USS New York* with 40 per cent more horsepower and an additional 2–14in guns.

The hull form was partly based on *Kongo*'s, with a long forecastle deck, a low quarterdeck, and secondary guns in casemates. Without the need for the massive machinery plant required for a battlecruiser's high speed, it was about 40ft shorter. Armour protection was also considerably enhanced in keeping with her role as a battleship with thicker hull and turret armour so despite the shorter length, the overall displacement was some 2000 tons heavier than *Kongo*. With the design work complete, *Fuso* was laid down on 11 March 1912. She was to be the first battleship built in Japan using Japanese manufactured materials and weapons. Three sister ships were authorised, the first being *Yamashiro*, which was laid down in November 1913. She was to be completed to the same design as *Fuso*.

Financial difficulties prevented the laying down of the next two ships until 1915, which allowed time for some design improvements. The forecastle deck was shortened, the amidships turrets were grouped together and placed aft of the second funnel and the hull length was increased by 10ft to give more machinery space. The changes resulted in the two ships becoming known as the 'Improved *Fuso*' or *Ise* class. Both *Ise* and *Hyuga* were laid down in May 1915.

Armour. *Fuso* and *Yamashiro*: The armour scheme was extensive, totalling 8588 tons or 29 per cent of the ship's displacement. Running the length of the forecastle deck from No 1 barbette to No 5 and extending down one deck to the quarterdeck was a 6in armour belt providing protection behind the casemates. Below this belt, running from No 1 barbette to No 6 and extending down from the quarterdeck to several feet below the waterline was an 8in belt protecting the main magazines. Amidships between the foremast and the mainmast, the 8in belt thickened to 12in. This was the main belt of Vickers Cemented armour providing protection for the machinery spaces. This thicker belt started one deck below the quarterdeck, extending downwards below the waterline to the bottom of the adjacent 8in armour, where it thinned to 4in.

Armoured bulkheads 12in thick ran across the ship, joining the side armour belts to create the armoured box, or citadel, which protected the ship's vital areas. The bulkheads thinned to 4in below the waterline. The citadel featured 575 watertight compartments. Aft of No 6 barbette, the steering gear was protected by 4in of armour. Forward of No 1 barbette there was additional side armour from 4in to 5in thick.

Horizontal protection was very light in comparison. Consisting of a 1.25in layer on the forecastle deck and a 2in layer on the quarterdeck, it was of high tensile steel and not true armour plate. The turret barbettes were protected by armour varying between 8in and 12in. The main turrets had 12in faces, 8in sides, and 4.5in roofs. The conning tower had an 8in roof and 13.75in sides. The casemate guns had 3.5in armoured shields.

Ise and *Hyuga*: The armour scheme for these two ships was very similar to the *Fuso* class, with the hull plating, steering gear protection, and the horizontal armour being the same. The 6in casemate belt was shorter than in *Fuso* and the conning tower and main barbettes were protected by 12in armour on all sides. The horizontal armour was sloped at the sides and met the side belt at the lower edge instead of at the top edge as in *Fuso*. Total weight of armour was 9680 tons, 30 per cent of total displacement.

Anti-torpedo system. A very innovative feature of all four ships was an anti-torpedo bulkhead located 19in behind the main armour belt amidships. While not providing the same level of protection as the bulges added later during reconstruction, this did at least provide a barrier against flooding from any torpedo hit along the main armour belt.

Main armament. Capable of firing a 1485lb shell, the 14in/45 guns were designed by Vickers for the *Kongo* and adapted for the *Fuso* and *Ise* classes. The mountings themselves were based on the Vickers design supplied for *Kongo*, but were

Below: Fitting the gun barrels of turret No 4 aboard *Hyuga* during construction. The noticeable lack of any safety gear certainly speaks to the times. *(By courtesy of Ray Bean)*

Right: *Hyuga* with minimal superstructure prior to any modifications. The lack of national ensign makes it likely this was taken on builder's trials in 1918. Judging by the amount of smoke, her engine room gang is working at full tilt. *(By courtesy of Ray Bean)*

more heavily armoured. Armour piercing, high explosive, and (from 1939) incendiary shells were carried. Maximum elevation was 30° giving a range of 30,400yds; loading was at a fixed angle of 5° with a firing cycle of 30–40 seconds at maximum elevation. Barrel life was estimated at 280 rounds. The turrets were numbered No 1 to No 6 starting at the bow.

Secondary armament. The secondary armament guns fitted aboard the four ships were not dual purpose, being for use against surface targets or to fire starshell illumination rounds. The original designs called for two single 14pdr guns to be fitted to the roof of each main turret, but they were never installed.

Below: *Ise* in 1927 showing additions to the foremast before it was rebuilt. The volume of smoke inundating the foretop makes it clear why funnel cowls were fitted. The deck mounted 5.5in gun can be seen abreast the funnel. The torpedo nets are still fitted, Japan being the last of the major powers to remove them from their capital ships. *(Author's collection)*

ARMAMENT CHARACTERISTICS

Weapon	Maximum Elevation	Horizontal Range (yards)	Vertical Range (feet)	Rate of Fire (rpm)	Shell Weight (pounds)
14in/45 Type 41	30°	30,400	N/A	1.5	1485
6in/50 Type 41	15°	15,400	N/A	5	100
5.51in/50 Type 3	20°	17,800	N/A	10	84

In *Fuso* and *Yamashiro* the secondary armament was the same gun as fitted to the *Kongo* class, the Vickers-designed 6in/50. Sixteen of these guns were placed in single 72-ton mounts located in casemates widely spaced along both sides of the hull below the forecastle deck. The maximum elevation was 15° giving a range of 15,400yds; barrel life was estimated at 500–600 rounds.

For *Ise* and *Hyuga* a new gun of Japanese design was developed: the 5.5in/50. The shell was lighter than the 6in/50, which eased loading and enabled a rate of fire twice that of the larger gun. The single mount was also lighter at 36 tons. In order to deliver the same weight of fire as *Fuso*, twenty guns, were carried in single mountings, ten on each side of the hull, eighteen in casemates below the forecastle deck with another two on the forecastle deck abreast the fore funnel in shielded mounts. Due to the shorter forecastle deck in the *Ise* class, the casemate guns were concentrated much closer together than in *Fuso*. Maximum range was 17,800yds at an elevation of 20°.

Torpedoes. All four ships carried six 21in torpedo tubes fitted well below the waterline in single mounts, three tubes per side. On both classes the tubes were widely separated; the first pair ahead of turret No 1, the second pair under the forward bridge structure, and third pair aft of the second funnel.

Propulsion. Both *Fuso* and *Yamashiro* were fitted with four direct-drive Brown-Curtis steam turbines rated at 40,000shp installed in two engine rooms. There were four propeller shafts; the inner pair driven from the high- and low-pressure turbines, the outer pair from the medium-pressure turbines. Steam was supplied from eight double-ended and sixteen single-ended boilers arranged in four boiler rooms. All the boilers were coal fired with supplementary oil sprayers. Boiler rooms 1 and 2 were forward of turret No 3, while boiler rooms 3 and 4 were aft of it. The two engine rooms were aft of No 4 turret. The separation of the two sets of boiler rooms resulted in two widely spaced funnels. *Fuso* reached 23 knots at 46,500shp on her trials on 29 August 1915; *Yamashiro* reached 23.3 knots at 47,730shp on her trials.

The main machinery in *Ise* and *Hyuga* was the same as utilised in *Fuso* with the exception of the Parsons steam turbines fitted to *Hyuga*. The grouping of turrets No 3 and No 4 together meant that all the boiler rooms could be placed ahead of turret No 3 with the engine rooms aft of turret No 4. This was a much more efficient layout than *Fuso*'s and resulted in the production of an extra 5000shp from the same machinery. The two funnels were much closer together as a result of this revised boiler room layout. *Ise* reached 23.64 knots on trials, while *Hyuga* managed to hit 24 knots on hers.

Fire Control. The main and secondary armament employed a director control system, whereby rangefinders would determine the target's range and bearing and send the data to a central station where they would be combined with other factors such as the firing ship's speed and fall of shot to calculate the angle and elevation for the guns. The main armament was controlled by two directors, one at the top of the foremast and the other on the after control position built around the mainmast. The secondary armament had six directors: two on the foremast and four on the after control position. As a backup for the main directors, turret No 2 carried a 13ft rangefinder, while turrets 3, 4, and 5 were fitted with 15ft rangefinders.

Directors for the torpedoes and anti-aircraft guns were also carried on the foremast and the after control position. Various platforms were also required for spotting the fall of shot, for controlling the searchlights, and for command and tactical control. This led to a very complex arrangement of directors and associated observation and control platforms on the foremast bridge structure. Eventually so many platforms were added to the foremast as a result of refits that its basic tripod structure was no longer visible. The foremast was rebuilt in all four ships by the end of the 1920s, and then completely replaced with the characteristic pagodas during reconstruction in the 1930s.

A critical consideration was the ability to outrange any potential opponent, so the primary main battery director was required to be at least 123ft above the waterline. The maximum range of the main armament was increased during upgrades, which required heavier and larger directors to be placed ever higher to incorporate the optics needed to target effectively out to the longer ranges. The end result of this process was the development of the massive and complex pagoda-style bridges found on all Japanese battleships, the extreme examples of which were the ungainly structures carried by *Fuso* and *Yamashiro*.

Fire control had originally been developed in conjunction with the British, but when the Anglo-Japanese Naval Treaty was cancelled in the aftermath of the Washington Treaty in 1922, fire control development in Japan fell behind. However, in 1926, Britain supplied updated fire control tables for *Kongo*, and these were

Below: *Yamashiro* on 22 October 1930 at Kobe, just prior to reconstruction with rebuilt foremast, searchlight towers on the after funnel, and funnel cowl. The carrier in the background is *Kaga*. *(By courtesy of Ray Bean)*

COMPARISON OF *FUSO* WITH CONTEMPORARY DESIGNS

Ship	Laid Down	Completed	Length	Armament	Full Load	shp	Speed	Armour – Belt	Armour – Deck	Armour – Turret	Armour – CT
Fuso	11 Mar 1912	8 Nov 1915	673ft	12 x 14in	35,900	40,000	23	12–4in	2in–1.25in	12in	13.75in
Viribus Unitis	16 Jan 1912	Jul 1914	469ft	12 x 12in	22,000	25,000	20.5	11–8in	2.5in	11in	11in
Bretagne	1 Jul 1912	Sep 1915	541ft	10 x 13.4in	28,500	43,000	21	10.75in–7.25in	2.75in–1.5in	13in	11.75in
König	Oct 1911	Aug 1914	580ft	10 x 12in	28,148	31,000	21	14–10in	4.5in	14in	14in
Iron Duke	30 May 1912	Oct 1914	580ft	10 x 13.5in	30,380	29,000	21	12–4in	2.5in–1in	11in	11in
Caio Duilio	24 Feb 1912	May 1915	554ft	13 x 12in	24,715	32,000	22	9–8in	1.5in	9in	12in
Imperatritsa Maria	Oct 1911	Jul 1915	551ft	12 x 12in	24,000	26,500	21	12–4in	3in–1.5in	12in	12in
Nevada	4 Nov 1912	Mar 1916	583ft	12 x 14in	28,900	26,500	20.5	13.5–8in	3in–1.5in	18in	16in

COMPARISON OF *ISE* WITH CONTEMPORARY DESIGNS

Ship	Laid Down	Completed	Length	Armament	Full Load	shp	Speed	Armour – Belt	Armour – Deck	Armour – Turret	Armour – CT
Ise	6 May 1915	5 Dec 1917	683ft	12 x 14in	36,500	45,000	23.5	12–4in	2in–1.25in	12in	12in
Bayern	29 Sep 1913	Oct 1916	560ft	8 x 15in	28,000	52,000	22.5	13.75–6in	4.75in	13.75in	13.75in
Royal Sovereign	15 Jan 1914	May 1916	580ft	8 x 15in	31,200	40,000	23	13–11in	3–1in	13in	11in
New Mexico	14 Oct 1915	May 1918	624ft	12 x 14in	33,500	27,500	21	14–8in	3.5in	18in	16in

used to develop home-grown tables for the rest of the battle fleet that could target out to 43,740 yards; but the system was heavy and relied on manual inputs.

Estimates indicated that the Japanese Navy outranged the US battle fleet on average 4300yds to 5400yds after increases to the elevation of the main guns and the development of special shells. Targets could be tracked at 44,000yds and fire could be opened at 37,000yds. In 1939 it was claimed that accuracy was 12 per cent at ranges of 35,000 yards, but this was never put to the test in fleet manoeuvres and in practice the quality of Japanese battleship gunnery turned out to be very poor in the Pacific War. To give just one example, *Hiei* and *Kirishima* fired 297 14in shells at the destroyer USS *Edsall* in broad daylight on 1 March 1942 and scored just one hit.

Fuso completed without her main director on the foretop; it was installed in 1917.

Construction. *Fuso* was laid down at Kure Naval Yard on 11 March 1912 as Battleship 3. *Yamashiro* followed on 20 November 1913 at Yokosuka Navy Yard as Battleship 4. *Fuso* was launched on 28 March 1914 and completed on 8 November 1915, taking 43 months to build. *Yamashiro* was launched on 3 November 1915 and completed 18 months after *Fuso* on 31 March 1917 in a slightly less elapsed time of 41 months.

Because of delays with funding, *Ise* and *Hyuga* were not started until 1915 and were built in private yards rather than the government-run naval yards. *Ise* was laid down as Battleship 5 on 10 May 1915 at the

Fuso in 1925 after the first reconstruction of the foremast. The once simple tripod foremast has almost completely disappeared behind the many additional platforms. The gap between turret No 2 and the bridge structure can be clearly seen. *(Drawing by George Richardson)*

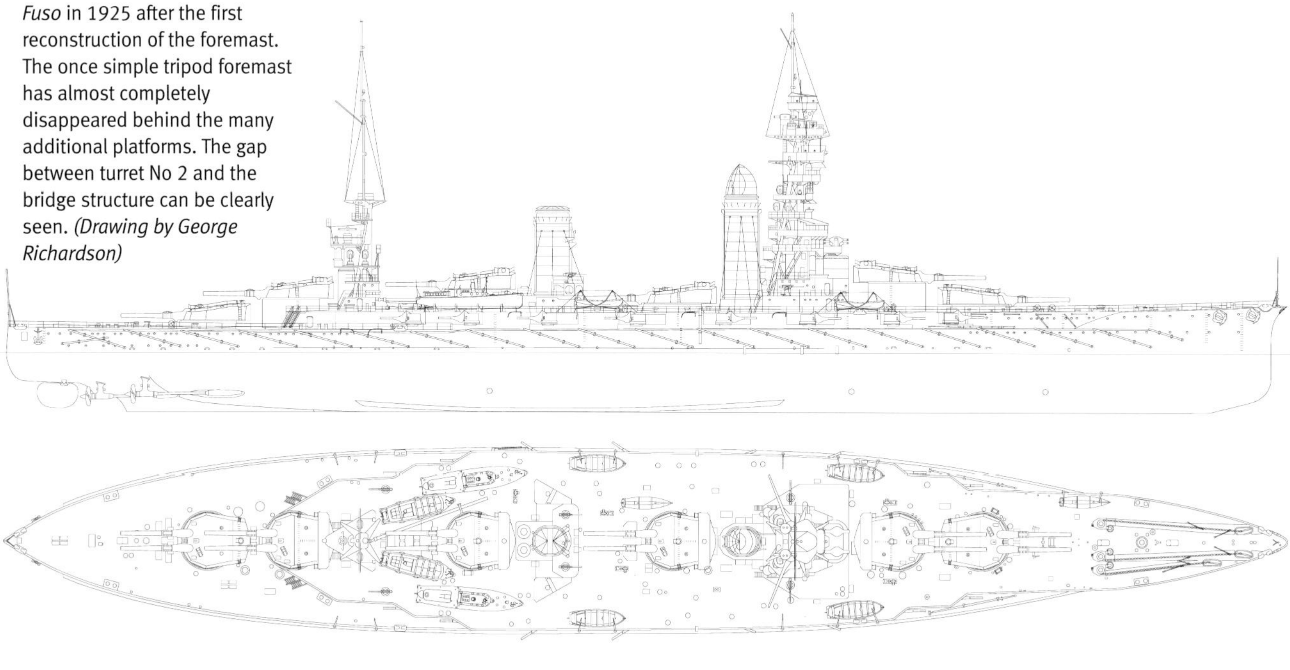

Left: *Hyuga* in 1931 with rebuilt foremast and funnel cowl. The torpedo nets and booms have been removed but the support shelf is still present. An aircraft can be seen atop turret No 5. *(By courtesy of Ray Bean)*

Left: *Ise* on trials before completing reconstruction, 8 December 1936. The foremost casemate gun has been removed. The twin 5in guns can be seen; the 25mm AA platforms have yet to be fitted. *(By courtesy of Ray Bean)*

Kawasaki Kobe yard, launched on 12 November 1916, and completed on 5 December 1917, taking only 32 months to build. *Hyuga*, Battleship 6, was laid down on 6 May 1915 at Mitsubishi Nagasaki, launched on 27 January 1917 and completed 30 April 1918. Her building time was 36 months.

At the time of completion, *Fuso* was among the world's largest and most powerful battleships although her overall protection was among the weakest.

By the time *Ise* and *Hyuga* were completed 2½ years later, they lagged considerably behind their contemporaries in every category; such was the speed of naval innovation during the First World War.

Left: *Fuso* undergoing post-reconstruction trials, 10 May 1933. The great height above the deck of the 5in guns on the after control position is evident, as is the soaring height of the bridge pagoda. Note that turret No 3 with its catapult is stowed facing forward. Author's collection)

SUMMARY OF CHARACTERISTICS AS BUILT

	Fuso Class	*Ise* Class
Displacement (Full Load)	35,900	36,500
Dimensions	Length 673ft, Beam 94ft, Draught 28ft 6in	Length 683ft, Beam 94ft, Draught 29ft 1in
Armament	12 – 14in/45, 16 – 6in/50, 6 – 21in TT	12 – 14in/45, 20 – 5.5in/50, 6 – 21in TT
Armour (maximum thickness)	Belt 12in, Deck 2in, Barbettes 12in Turrets: 12in face, 8in sides, 4.5in roof CT: 13.75in	Belt 12in, Deck 2in, Barbettes 12in Turrets: 12in face, 8in sides, 4.5in roof CT: 12in
Machinery	4 steam turbines = 40,000shp 24 mixed coal/oil-fired boilers	4 steam turbines = 45,000shp 24 mixed coal/oil-fired boilers
Range	8000nm @ 14 knots	9680nm @ 14 knots
Top Speed	23 knots	23.5 knots

CRITICISM OF THE DESIGN

***Fuso* and *Yamashiro*.** Despite the great weight of armour, the majority of it along the hull sides was only 6in or 8in thick and not proof against 14in shellfire. The deck protection was not actual armour plate and would have been easily penetrated by long-range plunging fire. The torpedo tube warheads were actually outside the armoured citadel and if detonated by a shell hit, the damage would have been severe if not catastrophic.

By choosing the twin turret, the designers committed themselves to a long hull which proved impossible to adequately protect. The US Navy adopted the triple 14in turret and fitted subsequent designs with four of them, giving the same firepower as *Fuso* but on a shorter and better protected hull. The Royal Navy shifted to the 15in gun in twin turrets, also on shorter and better protected hulls.

The location of amidships turrets Nos 3 and 4 was not ideal. The magazines were surrounded by the machinery spaces and required elaborate heat shielding and special cooling systems due to the heat generated by the power plant. The firing arcs were severely limited due to the bridge tower, funnels, and after control position. The wide dispersal of the main turrets did isolate them from each other in the event of damage, but there were very few spots for additional AA guns on the upper decks that were not affected by blast.

The loading and recoil systems used hydraulic pumps that were too small, which resulted in slow cycle times. To improve the rate of fire, the main guns were only fired one barrel at a time. The hydraulic system was also prone to leakage; the crews in the lower parts of the turrets had to wear rain-coats to keep dry.

The 6in battery extended too far forward with the result that forward guns were frequently awash and unusable. The guns abreast turrets No 3 and No 4 were badly affected by blast.

***Ise* and *Hyuga*.** The re-positioning of No 3 and No 4 turrets and lengthening the hull resolved the issues with firing arcs, blast, magazine cooling, and gave a more efficient machinery layout. The problems with armour protection remained, however. The secondary battery was also too far forward with the forward mounts frequently awash. The forecastle deck in this class was much shorter than *Fuso*'s, which cut down on crew space and as a result the two ships were regarded as the worst in the Japanese Navy for habitability.

RECONSTRUCTION

All four ships were extensively rebuilt in the 1930s, taking on the familiar form in which they fought the Pacific War. Full details of these reconstructions are given in the Appearance section, beginning on page 49.

Below: *Hyuga* on 4 December 1940. Note the position of the main topmast, ahead of the mainmast. The forward 5.5in casemate gun has been removed. *(By courtesy of Ray Bean)*

Careers

PRE-WAR

The four ships were completed between November 1915 and April 1918, but none of them saw action in the First World War. During the 1920s and 1930s they mainly operated in home waters or off the coasts of China, Manchuria, and Korca in support of military operations. The four ships were out of service for lengthy periods during the 1930s when they were reconstructed.

The first successful shipborne launch of an aircraft in the Japanese Navy took place aboard *Yamashiro* on 29 March 1922 whcn a Sparrowhawk fighter took off from her launching platform located on No 2 turret. *Yamashiro* scored another aviation 'first' in the spring of 1941 when radio-controlled Kawanishi E7K2 ('Alf') floatplanes were catapulted off and made successful flights.

1941

In November all four ships were stationed at the fleet anchorage of Hashirajima where they formed BatDiv 2 of the First Fleet under the command of Vice Admiral Takasu Shiro in his flagship *Ise*. Other than a one-week cruise south to the Bonin Islands from December 8 in company with *Nagato*, *Mutsu*, and the aircraft carrier *Hosho* providing distant support for the returning Pearl Harbor strike force, the opening month of the war was spent on 'standby alcrt' in or ncar thc fleet anchorage of Hashirajima.

1942

Fuso, *Ise* and *Hyuga* sortied on 12 March in response to the Marcus Island raid by the

Below: Sparrowhawk launching from *Yamashiro*'s No 2 turret on 29 March 1922, one of three practice launches that day. Note the single rangefinder fitted on the conning tower roof. The bridge has been glassed in. *(Author's collection)*

Right: Around 1930, a Yokosuka E1Y Type 14 floatplane fighter almost at flying speed with *Hyuga* in the background. *Hyuga*'s aircraft can be seen atop No 5 turret. Aircraft carried at this time had to be lowered over the side for take-off. The searchlight tower on the after funnel has been fitted. *(By courtesy of Ray Bean)*

USS *Enterprise* on 4 March, but no contact was made. The Doolittle raid on April 18 elicited a much speedier reaction from the Imperial Navy; BatDiv 2 sailed immediately in pursuit of the attacking Americans, but apart from stopping the neutral Russian freighter *Angarstroi*, the operation was uneventful.

On 5 May, during gunnery practice, a major explosion occurred in the breech of the left side gun in *Hyuga*'s turret No 5. The gun was totally destroyed and the turret roof was blown off, coming to rest on the upper deck. A major fire broke out, engulfing the turret and only the immediate flooding of the magazines averted a catastrophic detonation. The stricken *Hyuga* returned to Kure for emergency repairs. Not to be outdone, *Ise* suffered the complete flooding of No 2 engine room six days later due to faulty intake valves. She followed her sister ship to Kure for repairs.

The shattered remains of *Hyuga's* turret were removed and replaced with an armoured plate fitted with four triple 25mm mounts. There was no time for further work as BatDiv 2 sailed on 29 May for their part in the Midway operation as screen for the Aleutian Force. None of the ships saw action during the subsequent Midway debacle and they returned to Yokosuka on 14 June where they remained for the rest of the year on 'standby alert' and conducting training exercises.

Below: Inter-war exercises aboard *Ise* or *Hyuga*: turrets No 5 and No 6 are trained to starboard while her sister ship astern has just fired. Note the lattice structure atop the turret used to carry aerials aft. The metal straps on the gun barrels are where sub-calibre guns were fitted for shooting practice. *(By courtesy of Ray Bean)*

1943

The new year found BatDiv 2 still on 'standby alert' and conducting training and battle exercises. *Ise* was taken in hand in February for her conversion to carrier-battleship; *Hyuga* followed in May.

In August *Fuso* finally headed for the war zone. Loaded with troops and supplies and in company with battleships *Yamato* and *Nagato*, she sailed for Truk where she would be based for the remainder of the year. In October she sortied with the main fleet units to Eniwetok in response to radio intelligence suggesting a raid by US carriers on Wake Island. No contact was made with US forces.

Yamashiro was reclassified a gunnery training ship and spent the first ten months of the year on training exercises. In October she and the newly converted *Ise* were designated as the T-3 Transport group. Loaded with troop reinforcements, supplies, and main armament shells for *Fuso*, *Nagato*, and *Yamato*, the two battleships sailed for Truk on 15 October. After unloading, *Yamashiro* and *Ise* left Truk for Japan on 31 October in company with aircraft carriers *Junyo* and *Unyo*.

In the early morning of 5 November, in the first of a string of encounters between

Left: *Fuso* on 27 April 1939 in Sukumo Bay, island of Shikoku. The forward casemate gun has been removed and the catapult on No 3 turret is still in place. A 32ft rangefinder is fitted to the top of the bridge pagoda. *(By courtesy of Ray Bean)*

the four battleships and US submarines, USS *Halibut* made contact with the Japanese force as it began its transit of the Bungo Channel between the home islands of Shikoku and Kyushu. *Halibut* managed to fire eight torpedoes, one of which hit *Junyo* in the stern, disabling her rudder, and another hit *Yamashiro* but did not explode. *Junyo* was towed to safety; no other Japanese ship was damaged.

Hyuga's conversion was finished in November and together with *Ise* she spent the rest of the year on work-ups and trials. *Yamashiro* reverted to her role as gunnery training ship.

1944

The year opened with *Yamashiro*, *Ise*, and *Hyuga* in home waters and *Fuso* at Truk as part of the Combined Fleet.

On 1 February *Fuso* and the other units of the Combined Fleet evacuated Truk in the face of impending US airstrikes, moving to the anchorage at Lingga Roads, south of Singapore. US submarines *Permit* and *Puffer* sighted the Japanese ships but were unable to attack. *Fuso* remained at Lingga until May undergoing training and battle exercises.

On 11 May the Combined Fleet shifted anchorage to Tawi Tawi off the NE coast of Borneo. From there *Fuso* sortied on 30 May to take part in Operation Kon, the reinforcement of Biak Island off the coast of New Guinea. Sighted by US submarines *Fuso* nevertheless managed to make port safely at Davao in southern Mindanao on 31 May. On 2 June she sailed for Biak where she was to bombard Allied positions in support of a Japanese counter-landing. The operation was cancelled after the force was sighted and unsuccessfully bombed by US Army B-24s.

On 17 June American forces invaded Saipan in the Marianas. *Fuso* remained at Davao and took no part in the subsequent defeat of the Japanese Mobile Fleet in the

Below: *Yamashiro* dressed overall at Yokohama on 11 October 1940. Her pagoda bridge was much larger at its base than *Fuso*'s, as can be seen here. Her catapult has been landed. The cruiser *Suzuya* is visible over the stern. *(By courtesy of Ray Bean)*

Right: *Hyuga* converted to a carrier-battleship, shown at sea prior to the flight deck being fitted with sponsons for 25mm AA mounts. The main director atop the bridge pagoda is painted white. *(By courtesy of Ray Bean)*

Battle of the Philippine Sea. Desperate to land troop reinforcements, Combined Fleet HQ came up with a plan to have *Fuso* and *Yamashiro* make a counter-landing on Saipan. *Yamashiro* was quickly outfitted with landing barges and *Fuso* ordered to stand by for the sortie to Saipan. On sober reflection CinC Admiral Toyoda vetoed the plan, calling it a suicide mission doomed to failure, effectively just postponing what was to come for *Fuso* and *Yamashiro*.

Ordered back to Kure on 1 July, en route *Fuso* narrowly escaped the attentions of the US submarines *Robalo* and *Pomfret*, the latter firing six torpedoes, which all missed. *Yamashiro* became the new flagship of BatDiv2 when Vice Admiral Nishimura Shoji embarked in early September. On 23 September *Fuso* and *Yamashiro* sailed from Kure for Lingga Roads carrying 2000 troops, many of whom were billeted in tents on deck. During the operation the force was unsuccessfully attacked by the submarine USS *Plaice* and later sighted by *Pomfret* and *Flasher* but neither was able to close to make an attack. Both battleships arrived safely at Lingga on 4 October, but later transferred with the fleet to Brunei in response to the US landings at Leyte in the Philippines.

Ise and *Hyuga* were assigned to Carrier Division 4 with the aircraft carriers *Junyo* and *Ryuho*, the division's combined air group being designated Air Group 634. Workups and equipment trials occupied the first eight months of 1944. Despite many teething problems with the prototypes, by the end of August catapult trials of the Aichi E16A Zuiun ('Paul') seaplanes and the Yokosuka D4Y ('Judy') had been conducted successfully, along with shore-based training flights. Air Group 634 attained a limited operational status by October; continued difficulties with the aircraft hampered training efforts.

On 12 October US Task Force 38 began

Below: Carrier-battleship *Ise* on trials in late 1943 or 1944. The casemate guns have all been removed, while the sponsons for the flight deck 25mm guns have not yet been fitted. The main director and its Type 21 radar mattress are painted white. Note what appears to be a 'Val' on the flight deck with another partially visible on the port side. *(By courtesy of Ray Bean)*

Left: Artist's impression of *Yamashiro* under way as she would have appeared in the 1938–1942 time period. She presents a clean appearance with decks as yet uncluttered by light AA weapons. *(Koichi Shibata)*

an intense series of air raids on Formosa. Encouraged by wild and completely false claims of success against the US fleet, Air Group 634 along with Japan's remaining naval aviation groups were staged to Formosa to engage in the battle, where they were completely destroyed. This left Carrier Division 4 without aircraft for the upcoming decisive battle for the Philippines.

American forces landed on Suluan Island in Leyte Gulf on 17 October; this triggered Operation Sho-I-Go, the all-out defence of the Philippines. While a diversionary force composed of the last of Japan's operational aircraft carriers would attempt to lure US forces away from the beaches, Combined Fleet's battleships would proceed through the central Philippines to fall on the beachhead and annihilate the US transport fleet. It would be the largest naval battle in history.

THE BATTLE OF SURIGAO STRAIT

At Brunei on 21 October Admiral Nishimura was informed that his battleships were to be detached from the main force in order to make their way separately to Leyte Gulf from the south via Surigao Strait. The main force would proceed via San Bernardino Strait and approach Leyte Gulf from the north. Left unsaid at this last-minute change of plan was the suicidal nature of Nishimura's task as he would face the defending US forces alone in hopes of drawing them away from the main force.

The main force, including battleships *Yamato* and *Musashi*, sortied from Brunei at 07:45 on 22 October. Designated Force 'C', *Fuso*, *Yamashiro*, heavy cruiser *Mogami*, and four destroyers sailed at 15:30. Two days later, at 08:55 on October 24, Force 'C' was attacked by aircraft from the USS *Enterprise*. *Fuso* was hit by two bombs, one landing beside turret No 2 tearing a large hole in the deck and starting a fire. The second bomb detonated on the aircraft deck at the stern. The resulting fire destroyed both of her floatplanes and burnt out compartments immediately below. *Yamashiro* was near-missed very close to starboard, tearing open the seam between the hull and the starboard torpedo blister. At one point listing close to 12°, the flooding was brought under control and trim restored by counter-flooding. *Fuso*'s fires were out within 25 minutes. Force 'C' was battered but continued on.

Force 'C' was sailing into a deadly trap. Six battleships, eight cruisers, and twenty-three destroyers lay in wait, deployed at the northern end of Surigao Strait and along its eastern and western edges. Thirty-nine PT boats in three-boat sections were deployed at the southern end of the Strait and far out into the Bohol Sea. These were the first to attack, from 22:30, but no damage had been done to Force 'C' by 02:02, when it turned north into Surigao Strait in single file with the destroyers leading *Yamashiro*, *Fuso*, and *Mogami*

At 02:58 the first US destroyers began launching torpedoes at Force 'C' and at

Below: Artist's impression of *Ise* at sea in October 1944. The additional sponsons on the flight deck for the 25mm AA mounts and the 4.7in rockets have been fitted. *(Koichi Shibata)*

Above: Battleship *Fuso* and cruiser *Mogami* under aerial attack by American aircraft in the Sulu Sea, 24 October 1944. The smoke from the fire raging on *Fuso*'s aircraft deck at the stern is clearly visible. *(Author's collection)*

Below: *Yamashiro* under air attack in the Sulu Sea on 24 October 1944. While she was not hit during this attack, near-misses opened seams in her starboard torpedo blister. *(Author's collection)*

03:09 observers aboard *Mogami* saw two towering columns of water erupt from *Fuso*'s starboard side as at least two torpedoes struck home. Rapid flooding of the boiler rooms ensued and a fire broke out aft. *Fuso* swung out of line to starboard but continued making her way northwards at greatly reduced speed. Ten minutes later water began washing over the forecastle as the flooding proceeded unchecked. More US destroyers launched torpedoes and at 03:20 three of the Japanese destroyers were hit. *Yamashiro* was also hit on the port quarter and a fire broke out. The magazines for turrets No 5 and No 6 were flooded as a precaution, putting them out of action. The scene was chaotic as ships from both sides fired furiously at each other, tracers arced out of the night, star shells burst overhead, and searchlight beams snapped out into the

darkness. At 03:30 Admiral Nishimura sent out his last message giving a situation report. One minute later *Yamashiro* was hit by another torpedo on the port side, bringing her almost to a halt. Heroic damage control work had her back up to 18 knots within 5 minutes.

By now far astern, *Fuso* had come to a southerly heading, perhaps in an attempt to beach the ship. At 03:40, with her bow now under the water and with a very heavy list, the pagoda tower twisted and collapsed. The ship rapidly heeled over to starboard, capsizing and sinking by the bow. The last thing to be seen was her stern high in the air with the propellers still turning. As she slid under, the fire on the quarterdeck ignited the oil now spilling up from ruptured tanks and a huge oil fire broke out on the surface. There were only ten survivors.

Up to now the only US ships firing had been the destroyers, but at 03:51 USS *Louisville* opened fire on *Yamashiro*, quickly followed by the rest of the cruisers and at 03:53 by the battleships. Staggering into the maelstrom of shellfire, *Yamashiro* was pummelled by repeated hits and fires broke out throughout her entire length, blazing from the waterline to the top of the pagoda. She was hit by another torpedo at 04:05.

Yamashiro's main guns took cruisers *Phoenix* and *Shropshire* under fire while her secondary batteries were engaging the US destroyers, which were firing from everywhere. *Yamashiro*'s fire was very accurate, suggesting some sort of radar control still in use. After the US destroyer *Albert W Grant* came under friendly fire as well as being hit by *Yamashiro*, cease fire was ordered at 04:09 aboard the US ships until the situation could be clarified. The sudden darkness and quiet was illuminated by the fires now raging on *Yamashiro* and *Mogami*, both of which turned to the south.

At 04:19 *Yamashiro* was hit by another torpedo and came to an abrupt halt. A port list rapidly developed and the pagoda mast collapsed to port. Two minutes later, with 'deadly suddenness', she capsized and sank stern first. Just like her sister, she left only ten survivors. Almost 4000 crew members perished with the two ships.

In April 2001 the John Bennett Deep Ocean Research International Company located a wreck believed to be *Yamashiro* near her recorded sinking position in the Surigao Strait at a depth of about 600 feet. The wreck appears to be largely intact.

THE BATTLE OFF CAPE ENGAÑO

On 20 October *Ise* and *Hyuga*, with no planes embarked, sailed from the Inland Sea as part of Vice Admiral Ozawa's Diversionary Force along with aircraft carriers *Zuikaku*, *Zuiho*, *Chitose*, and *Chiyoda*. On October 24 air strikes from the carriers were launched against US forces

Left: *Ise* under attack during the Battle off Cape Engaño, 25 October 1944. Note turrets No 3 and No 4 trained to starboard and both catapults swung out. The rocket launchers on their sponsons on the flight deck can also be seen. The main topmast is *behind* the mainmast, a sure identification feature for *Ise*. *(By courtesy of Ray Bean)*

operating further south. *Ise* and *Hyuga* were detached to scout ahead and possibly make a night attack but were recalled late in the day after having been spotted.

At 07:13 on the morning of 25 October *Hyuga's* Type 13 air search radar picked up enemy aircraft at a range of 105 miles. *Ise* tracked further incoming aircraft at 125 miles. The various radar sets functioned well, continuing to track incoming US aircraft all day, but to no avail. With no aircraft left aboard and the few defending fighters quickly shot down, the Diversionary Force was decimated by all-day air attacks from TF38 that began at 08:30. All four carriers, the cruiser *Tama*, and two destroyers were sunk or left dead in the water. Both battleships came under heavy attack, *Ise* avoiding eleven torpedoes but was near-missed by as many as thirty-four bombs which opened up her hull plates and caused minor flooding. *Hyuga* also suffered flooding from near-misses. Both ships used their main armament to shoot back at the attacking planes.

In the early evening, the submarine USS *Halibut* fired six torpedoes at *Hyuga* which all missed. For a time in the evening, *Ise* and *Hyuga* proceeded to the south in hopes of engaging US surface forces that were polishing off crippled and damaged Japanese ships. They failed to make contact and retired to the northwards at 22 knots. Five submarines made contact with the fleeing Japanese ships with the USS *Sea Dog* getting close enough to fire torpedoes, which all missed. The remnants of the Diversionary Force reached Kure on 29 October.

On 11 November *Ise* and *Hyuga* sailed from Kure carrying troops and ammunition destined for Manila. After transhipping the supplies and troops to smaller vessels in the Spratly Islands on the 16th, they carried on to the south and reached Lingga Roads on 22 November. They were deployed to Camranh Bay, Indo-China in mid-December in hopes of intercepting a US convoy bound for Mindanao, but the operation was cancelled and both ships saw out the year at Lingga on 'standby alert'. While at Camranh Bay they were once again spotted by US submarines, but none of the subs was able to carry out an attack.

1945

There would be one last operation for the battleships as they were used to transport strategic materials to Japan from Singapore. In company with light cruiser *Oyodo* and three destroyers, they sailed on 10 February. Fully alerted to the operation, the Allied command deployed no less than twenty-six submarines along their projected track and Army Air Forces in the Philippines were ready to bomb the ships at sea. Nevertheless, by anchoring in protected harbours at night, maintaining a high speed of 22 knots, and aided by poor weather conditions, the ships all reached Japan unscathed ten days later.

Both ships were at Kure on 19 March when US forces launched major air attacks on the remnants of the Japanese fleet. *Ise* was hit by two bombs, and *Hyuga* by three, but both remained afloat and combat ready.

Below: *Ise* under heavy air attack and on fire fore and aft, 24 July 1945. Turrets 1 and 2 are sporting striped camouflage. *(Author's collection)*

Right: Overhead view of the wrecked *Ise*, showing the badly damaged flight deck. Three of the 5in mounts have been removed along with most of the 25mm AA guns. The rocket launchers are still in place. *(Author's collection)*

Below, left: Looking up at the starboard rear of *Hyuga*'s shattered bridge pagoda after her sinking. Note the Type 21 radar mattress trained to starboard. *(Author's collection)*

Below, right: The wreck of *Hyuga* sunk in shallow water with the devastated flight deck clearly evident. The sponsons for the 4.7in rocket launchers are visible right aft. *(US National Archives ID Code 80-G-490239)*

In April they were both camouflaged and towed to new sites near Kure where they functioned as AA batteries. The end came for both ships at the end of July as they came under heavy air attack beginning on the 24th. *Hyuga* was hit by ten bombs and near-missed by another thirty. Heavily on fire and with the bridge pagoda wrecked, over the next two days she gradually sank to the bottom on an even keel with her decks awash.

Ise was badly damaged by five direct hits and numerous near-misses during the same attacks but was not sunk. Her flooded compartments were pumped out and plans were made to get her to dry dock. Before that could be done, she was attacked again on 28 July. Hit by another eleven bombs, the damage proved too much for the ship and she sank with a 15° starboard list, settling on the bottom with her decks awash.

Ise was scrapped where she lay beginning in October 1946. *Hyuga* was raised prior to being scrapped. Both ships ceased to exist by July 1947.

Model Products

Despite their rather luck-lustre careers, these ships have proven to be extremely popular with modellers: no fewer than 46 kits were available at time of writing (2016) in scales ranging from 1:2400 to 1:250. The great majority are injection-moulded plastic, but there are also some very high quality resin and card kits available. The first 1:700 scale kits of the two classes were produced in the 1970s: Aoshima released *Fuso* and *Yamashiro*, Hasegawa releasing *Ise* and *Hyuga*. Once very much the state of the art, the original kits have been superseded with new toolings to reflect the growing sophistication of modellers.

There are many aftermarket accessories available for all four ships, ranging from simple etch sheets through wooden decks to boxed multi-media sets. Modellers will have no problems selecting accessories appropriate to their skill level and desired level of detail.

KONISHI *FUSO* 1:1250 Scale

Konishi is a scale model manufacturer of long standing based in Osaka, Japan. They have several different lines of model ships in various scales, the 1:1250 series is listed as 'Waterline Model Ships' on their website. Both of the *Fuso* class and the battleship and carrier-battleship versions of the *Ise* class are produced in this scale.

The 1:1250 model ships have a cast metal hull – somewhat sturdier than their European equivalents – and small parts made of brass, which normally include all of the superstructure, turrets, smaller guns, and planes. They are sold as complete, painted models and have to be ordered direct from Konishi as there are no authorised dealers.

The model of *Fuso* is representative of the Konishi production standards. The turrets on Konishi models are cemented in place and do not rotate.

Photos courtesy of **Jeffrey Stevenson**

Below: Konishi *Fuso* (Kit 114)

AOSHIMA *FUSO* 1944 or 1942 SUPER DETAIL 1:700 Scale

This 2007 kit is Aoshima's first re-tooling of *Fuso*, featuring many of the same components as the companion *Yamashiro* re-tooling with pieces for *Fuso*'s unique bridge pagoda and AA layout. Representing *Fuso* in August 1944 but without any single 25mm mounts, the kit components are well moulded with plenty of detail. There are a couple of minor issues: it has an awkward forecastle deck insert and the platform over the conning tower is too long and interferes with the AA mounts on turret No 2; it needs to be shortened or replaced.

Above: *Fuso* Super Detail box art

This packaging of the re-tooled kit has a couple of extra features: an option to build *Fuso* as she appeared in 1942, and a metal photo-etch sheet for extra detailing. The bulwarks for the deck edge 25mm guns are in the regular release of this kit, but this Super Detail version does not have them; they will need to be scratch-built

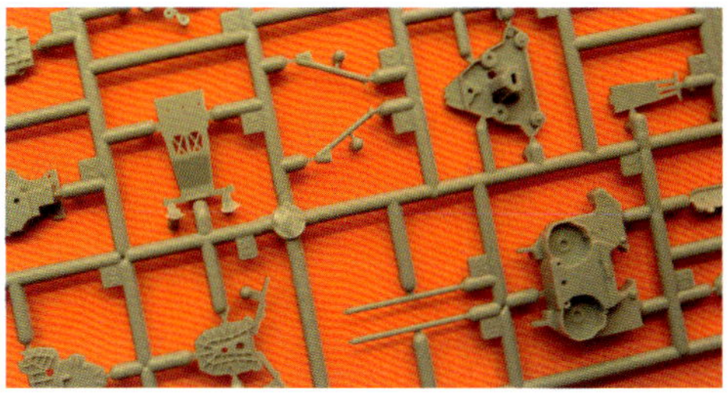

Left: Pagoda bridge parts showing the amount of moulded-in detail

if modelling the 1944 fit using this kit.

There is a separate instruction sheet for the 1942 *Fuso* which mainly requires leaving off all but eight twin 25mm mounts and the radars, but there is an extra piece for the amidships funnel platform. The photo-etch sheet includes aircraft trolleys, aircraft propellers, aircraft deck turntables, catapult, crane boom, funnel grille, search-light platform lattice supports, RDF loop, davits, and small boat cranes. It has its own instruction sheet but the modeller is left to figure out where the parts go on the model.

There are 164 parts on eleven kit-specific sprues along with the Japanese Navy Battleship Ordnance Set. Painting instructions with a profile and overhead view are on the standard instruction sheet.

Review kit courtesy of **Kraken Hobbies**

AOSHIMA *FUSO* 1938 — 1:700 Scale

Right: Box art for the *Fuso* 1938 kit

Below: *Fuso* 1938 kit contents

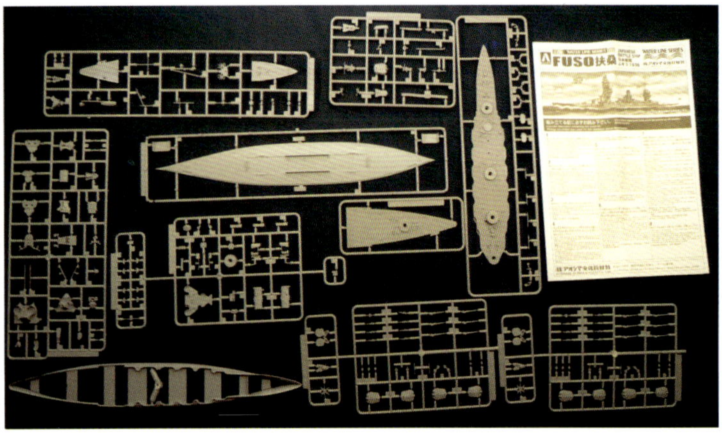

This kit was released in 2011 and accurately represents *Fuso* as she appeared between 1938 and 1941 with the catapult on the roof of No 3 turret and a higher pagoda than she carried in 1944. The turrets, funnel, searchlight platforms, aft control tower, and the lower pagoda have the same pieces as the *Fuso* Super Detail kit. The additional pagoda levels and extra bracing are included on a new sprue that also has a new No 3 turret, the cata-pult, aircraft elevator, and the aircraft handling derrick.

The one-piece hull is new, with separate forecastle and quarterdeck pieces which are full length without the troublesome inserts found in the first re-tooling. All of the new pieces and the new hull have the same high level of detail found in the earlier re-tooled kits from Aoshima. There are 169 parts on twelve kit-specific sprues along with the Japanese Navy Battleship Ordnance Set. The painting instructions are noted on the profile and overhead views in the set of instructions.

Review kit kindly lent by **imperialhobbies.ca**

AOSHIMA *FUSO* 1944 RETAKE — 1:700 Scale

Right: *Fuso* second retake quarterdeck detail

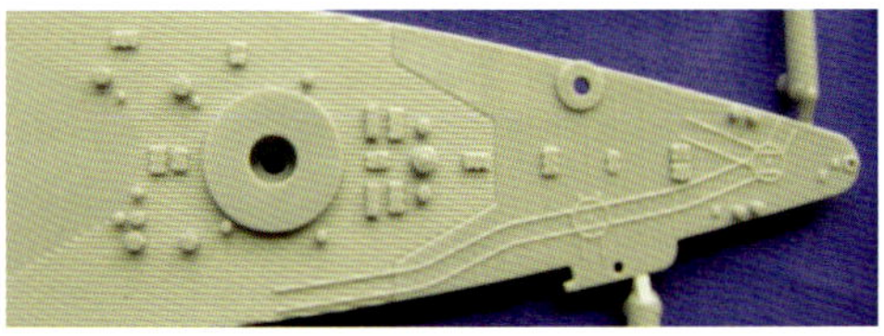

Below: *Fuso* 1944 second retake kit contents

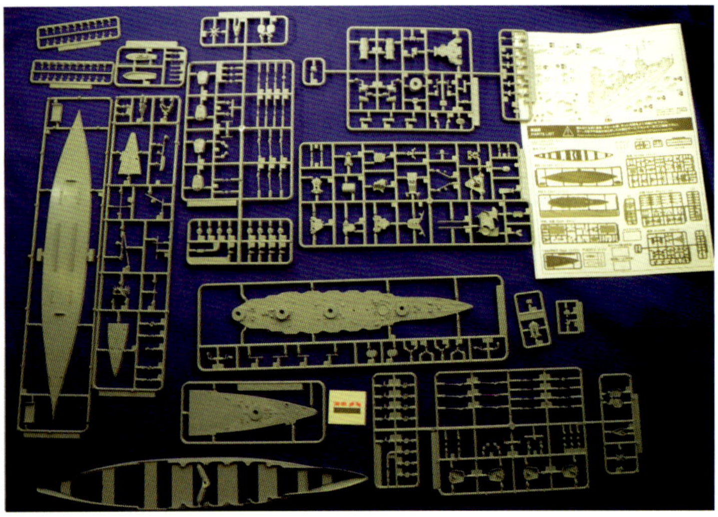

This 2015 kit is Aoshima's second re-tooling of *Fuso*. It uses many of the same parts as the first re-tooling, with new pieces for the bridge pagoda and searchlight platform and includes 40 single 25mm guns. The new hull and decks from the *Fuso* 1938 kit are used. *Fuso*'s aircraft deck did not extend under the barrels of turret No 6, and the quarterdeck piece matches that. The level of detailing is to the same high standards as the earlier re-tooling.

The new pieces and the 25mm singles make this kit a very accurate representa-tion of *Fuso* after her last refit in August 1944. Despite the increased level of accu-racy it still has the incorrect conning tower platform: a minor problem and easily corrected. There are 242 parts on nineteen kit-specific sprues along with the Japanese Navy Battleship Ordnance Set. It even includes an 8-piece PT boat.

The first re-tooling of *Fuso* is quite an impressive kit; this second re-tooling is equally as good and with a greater degree of accuracy. The painting instructions refer-ence the Mr Colour range and are found with the profile and overhead views in the instructions. An additional overhead view showing the placement of the 25mm singles is also shown.

Review kit courtesy of **Aoshima Models**

FUJIMI *FUSO* 1944

1:350 Scale

This very impressive kit of *Fuso* in her final configuration prior to her loss has 1037 parts on 26 sprues. As would be expected with such a large part count, the amount of detail is immense. The large size of the superstructure pieces makes possible high levels of moulded-in detail. The wood decks have individually scribed planks, metal decks have anti-skid patterns, and the bulkheads have hatches, scuttles, and life preservers. All the lattice structures are very thinly moulded and are see-through.

The full hull is split into port and starboard halves with well-defined degaussing cable, casemate openings, bilge keels, and the anti-torpedo bulge. Most of the scuttles are depicted as blanked off, with the exception of the uppermost row under the forecastle, which are open and feature rigols ('eyebrows'). The waterline is not marked, so the kit drawings will need to be consulted in order to correctly place it.

Above: Box art for Fujimi 1:350 *Fuso*

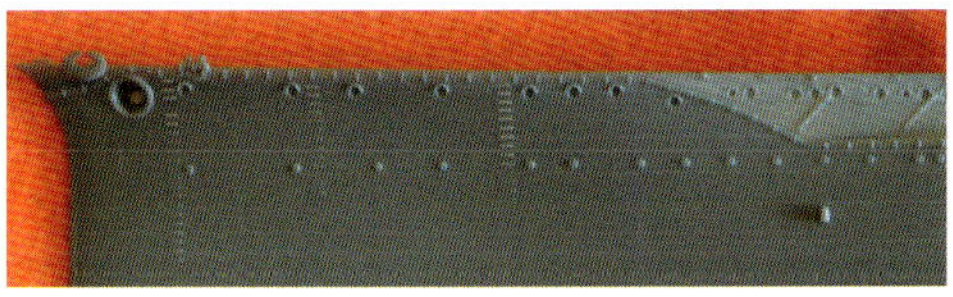

Left: Hull detail

The forecastle and quarterdeck are one very large piece, with the hatches, skylights, aircraft transport rails, and turntables moulded in place. Capstans, winches, vents, ready-use ammunition lockers, cable reels, and paravanes are individual parts, over 200 in all. Each of the five sub-assemblies for fitting these parts is accompanied by an overhead view showing precisely where each part is fitted.

The level of detail is carried over into the superstructure – 33 steps are required to assemble the bridge pagoda, and 16 for the funnel and searchlight platforms. The main and secondary armament feature individual gun barrels with the main armament gun barrels having drilled-out muzzles and separate blast bags. Ship's boats are highly detailed, featuring scribed planking and separate cabins and thwarts. The 25mm twin and triple mounts are made from four pieces, the single 25mm from two. The bridge windows, searchlights, and the single 'Pete' aircraft are moulded in clear plastic.

A 20-page booklet makes up the instructions. Port, starboard, fore, aft, and overhead drawings in 1:350 with paint swatches from the Mr Colour range are on a 31in x 21in full colour sheet. Anchor chain, a display stand, and decals for flags and aircraft markings are also included. The only minor criticism is the lack of the single 13.2mm guns that *Fuso* carried in October 1944; they need to be sourced elsewhere.

Review kit kindly lent by **Kerry Jang**

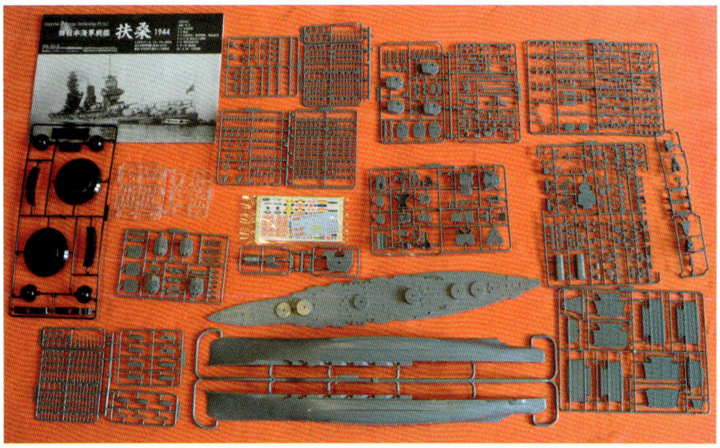

Below: Kit contents

DIGITAL NAVY *FUSO* 1935

1:250 Scale

This card model comes as a downloadable PDF file containing 29 pages of parts in full colour and represents *Fuso* in 1935, prior to the stern being lengthened and the side bulges raised to the quarterdeck level. Constructed from internal frames to which the hull plating is attached, it can be built either as full hull or waterline. Over 300 parts include three aircraft, ship's boats, and deck fittings and will assemble into an impressive 32.5in model. Ten pages of comprehensive and easy to follow instructions featuring exploded views and text are included.

An appealing feature of card models is that no painting is required leaving the modeller free to concentrate on assembly; the only additional task after building is complete is touching up any exposed card edges.

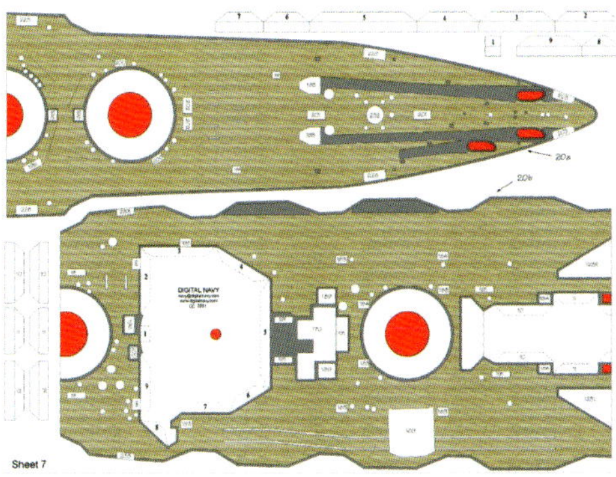

Left: Forecastle deck

Review kit courtesy of **Digital Navy**

VOYAGER MODEL *FUSO* MAIN GUN TURRET

1:144 Scale

This unique kit is of *Fuso*'s No 1 turret as it appeared in 1939. The one-piece turret is finely cast in resin with clearly defined blast bags, rivets, and raised plating on the turret roof. Two sighting hoods and the base make up the rest of the resin parts. The gun barrels are machined metal with the muzzles drilled out. A photo-etch sheet is provided with railings, ladders, a sighting hood cover, platforms for the gun barrels, and an engraved name plate. A double-sided set of instructions is included. With only 17 parts this will prove to be a quick build and an interesting addition to any model collection.

Review kit courtesy of **Kraken Hobbies**

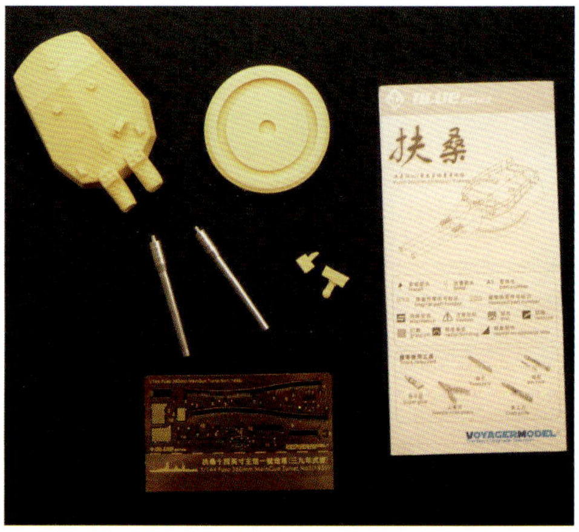

Right: Contents of the *Fuso* gun turret kit

AOSHIMA *YAMASHIRO* 1935

1:700 Scale

Once state of the art, this kit now shows just how far the hobby has progressed since its first release in the 1970s. With only two twin 25mm mounts, the kit is fairly close to representing *Yamashiro* immediately after her reconstruction in 1935.

This is not just a re-boxing of the associated *Fuso* kit, but includes the features that differentiated *Yamashiro* from her sister: the extra superstructure connecting turret No 2 to the bridge structure, the larger pagoda, and the heavier bracing at the back. The only real problem is the presence of the portside aircraft elevator amidships, a feature never fitted in *Yamashiro*. It could be removed easily as there is no deck detail in that area. There is some detail: the searchlight platforms around the funnel have separate supports, the funnel has a separate cap, the casemate guns have blast bags, and there are hatches, bollards, and capstans on the deck.

It is in the area of moulded-in detail where the kit suffers in comparison with the re-tooled releases. The gun turrets and bulkheads have no detail, the deck planks are much too wide, the boats are very simple and there are no davits or chocks for them, the bridge pagoda is very simplified, there is no aircraft deck, and the bridge windows are represented by a peel and stick decal.

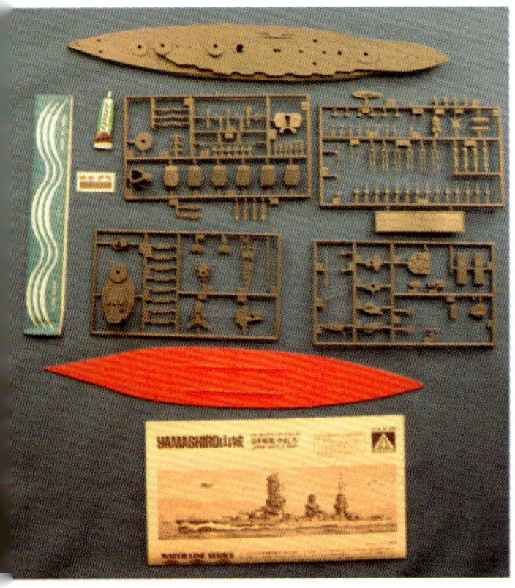

Above: Components of the kit with the included tube of glue. Note the one-piece hull and decks

Right: Box art of the original Aoshima *Yamashiro*

AOSHIMA *YAMASHIRO* 1944

1:700 Scale

This is the re-tooled kit released in 2007 representing *Yamashiro* after her final refit in August 1944, minus the single 25mm guns. The moulding is crisp with a high level of moulded-in detail, the decks featuring anchor chain, paravanes, hatches, bollards, capstans, and raised planking. The hull has raised lines for the plating strakes and incorporates the bulge and the V-shaped stern. The two-piece funnel has steam piping and a separate cap. The supports for the searchlight platforms around the funnel and the bracing for the pagoda are solid pieces, but the lattice work is well defined. The 25mm mounts on the main deck are in sandbagged positions. The main turrets are well detailed, with individual barrels that have

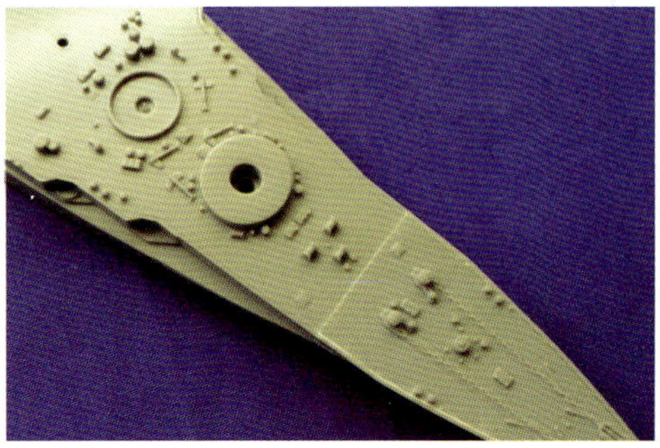

Right: Forecastle detail showing the troublesome seam

blast bags. The secondary guns also have blast bags. Windows on the bridge pagoda are moulded in.

The hull and decks are one piece with inserts for the forecastle and aircraft decks. The forecastle insert is awkwardly placed and the seam will be hard to hide. There are 162 parts on eight kit-specific sprues along with the Japanese Navy Battleship Ordnance Set. The instructions have a profile and overhead view with painting instructions.

AOSHIMA *YAMASHIRO* 1944 RETAKE 1:700 Scale

Released in 2014, this is Aoshima's second re-tooling of *Yamashiro*. A much more significant upgrade than *Fuso's* second re-tooling, this kit contains many new parts. There are more pieces for the after control tower and the searchlight platforms, the bracing on the back of the bridge pagoda has hollow cut-outs, and the pagoda itself has modified platforms and is one level shorter. The pieces that feature lattice are see-through and not solid. There are 40 single 25mm guns and a new funnel with separate steam pipes.

Left: Kit components of the Aoshima *Yamashiro*

The kit uses the new hull and forecastle deck from the *Fuso* 1938 kit; the quarter-deck piece has the slightly different shape of *Yamashiro*'s aircraft deck which extended under the barrels of turret No 6. A very well thought out upgrade, all the new parts make this a very accurate model of the ship after her last refit in August 1944.

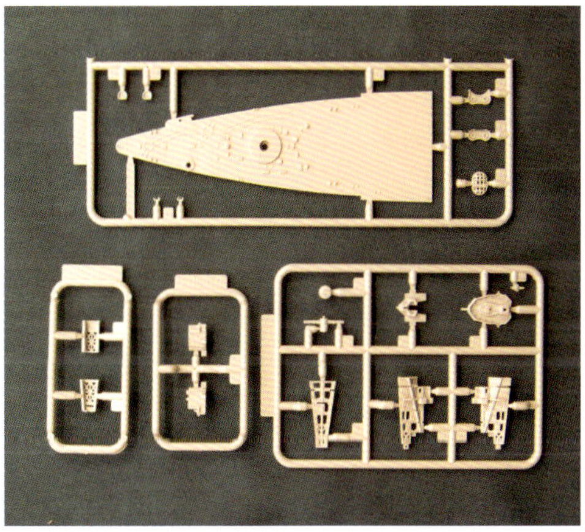

Left: Superstructure and quarterdeck pieces specific for *Yamashiro*

The new parts are on four new sprues, all with considerable moulded detail. The older parts from the first re-tooling are also included but not used – the instructions are quite clear about which parts to use. There are 331 parts on seventeen kit-specific sprues, but many of these are the older parts and will not be needed. The Japanese Navy Battleship Ordnance Set and a Surigao Strait nemesis PT boat are included. A profile and overhead view showing the positioning of the single 25mm guns and paint references for the Mr Colour range are in the instructions.

Review kit courtesy of **Aoshima Models**

HI-MOLD *YAMASHIRO* 1941 or 1944 1:700 Scale

This resin kit comes with two complete sets of instructions and alternate parts for building *Yamashiro* in either her 1941 or 1944 configuration. The one-piece hull is cast complete up to the forecastle deck, nicely capturing the complex hull shape forward and the V-shaped stern. The case-mate mounts, overhanging structure for the aircraft crane, degaussing cable, blanked off starboard forward anchor, and armour belt are all well-defined.

Above: The mixed media components of the kit

The deck features extremely sharp details: planking, anchor chain, cable reels, paravanes, capstans, bollards, and the aircraft deck with its transport rails and turntables. Cut-outs for fitting the main superstructure parts are also present. The pagoda platforms are on two resin wafers, the rest of the superstructure parts and the main gun turrets being cast individually. The pagoda platforms are detailed top and bottom with bulkhead features and bridge windows where appropriate. The single-piece funnel has external pipes and a well-defined funnel grille. The ships boat's are moulded with chocks.

Many of the smaller detail parts are in white metal: crane boom, secondary armament, 13mm singles, directors, pagoda bracing, catapult, masts, searchlights, anchors; all very high quality and well defined. Brass rod is supplied for the pagoda supports and there are twelve machined main armament gun barrels. Three sprues of Skywave plastic parts are included for the 25mm AA guns and aircraft. Each set of instructions features a parts list and exploded views of parts assembly. An overhead view showing the precise locations of all the AA guns is on the 1944 instructions. There are two sets of profile and overhead views with painting instructions.

Hi-Mold has a reputation for precision casting and this kit does not disappoint, the quality of casting and level of detail easily matching the best injection moulded plastic kits.

Right: Detail of the quarterdeck showing the level of detail cast into the kit

■ Review kit courtesy of **Kraken Hobbies**

HASEGAWA *ISE*/*HYUGA* 1937 — 1:700 Scale

These kits are the new tooled versions that were released in 2002 and depict *Ise* and *Hyuga* as they appeared after their reconstruction. The kit components are identical, the only difference being the assembly instructions for the mainmast topmast: at the rear of the mainmast for *Ise*, at the front for *Hyuga*.

Below: Components of the Hasegawa *Ise* kit

There are 134 parts on nine kit-specific sprues along with the Japanese Navy Battleship Ordnance Set. The hull is split into port and starboard halves which feature thinly scribed hull strakes and the anti-torpedo bulge. The forecastle and quarterdeck are separate pieces with plenty of moulded-in detail: anchor chain, paravanes, hatches, bollards, capstans, raised deck planking, and the aircraft deck. The supports for the searchlight platforms are solid pieces with well-defined lattice work. The main turrets have raised plating; the individual gun barrels feature blast bags, as do the secondary guns. The two-piece funnel has raised detail and a separate cap. Twelve superstructure pieces with moulded-in windows where appropriate make up the bridge pagoda.

A decal sheet with flags, ensigns, and aircraft markings is provided. The instructions have a profile and overhead view with painting instructions that reference the Mr Colour and Tamiya ranges.

Right: Box art of the Hasegawa *Hyuga* – Battleship version

HASEGAWA *ISE* HIGH GRADE SPECIAL — 1:700 Scale

This kit has the same components as the regular Hasegawa battleship version of *Ise* with numerous extras: an additional sprue moulded in red plastic with lower hull parts and display stands, white metal propellers, wooden display base, name plate, machined barrels for the main armament and a metal photo-etch sheet. The kit can be assembled without the lower hull as the hull base plate is included.

The etch sheet has replacement parts for the aircraft crane boom, aircraft propellers, aircraft trolleys, catapult, davits, funnel

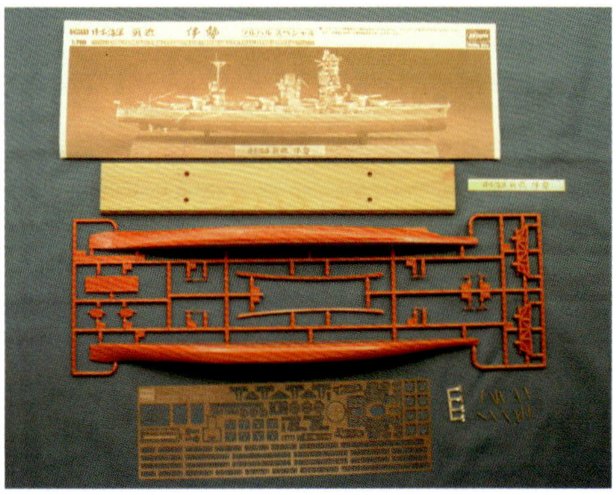

Right: The additional parts that make up the High Grade kit

grille, jackstaff, mainmast aerials, RDF loops, searchlight platform lattice supports, and the Type 21 radar. It also has accommodation ladders and pre-cut lengths of deck railing. The circular platform that replaced *Hyuga*'s turret No 5 is also present enabling that version to be modelled if desired.

The regular kit instructions are upgraded to include the assembly and placement of all the extra parts.

■ Review kit kindly lent by **Kerry Jang**

HASEGAWA *ISE*/*HYUGA* CARRIER-BATTLESHIP 1944

1:700 Scale

These kits depict *Ise* and *Hyuga* as they appeared during the Battle of Leyte Gulf in October 1944. Just as with the regular battleship version, these new tooled kits are also identical to each other except for the assembly of the mainmast topmast.

The hull and most of the superstructure is common between the regular battleship kit and this carrier version and features the same level of detail. This kit includes additional AA weapons and platforms, catapults, air group, and the parts for the hangar and flight deck. The air group consists of 8 'Judy' and 8 'Paul' seaplanes, all with panel lines. The flight deck has moulded-on transport rails and turntables; the rocket launchers have raised detail on the fronts. The elevator is a separate piece and the hangar sides even have slightly raised plating lines. No hangar interior detail is present; those wishing to position the elevator at hangar deck level will need to do some scratch-building. The bridge pagoda platforms have been modified slightly to accommodate extra AA mountings. All six main gun turrets are included, but no secondary armament.

There are 183 parts on twelve kit-specific sprues along with the Japanese Navy Battleship Ordnance Set. Decals for flags, ensigns, and aircraft markings along with painting instructions that reference the Mr Colour and Tamiya ranges are provided. The instructions also feature the usual overhead and profile drawings of the model.

Above: Box art of the Hasegawa *Ise* – Carrier-Battleship

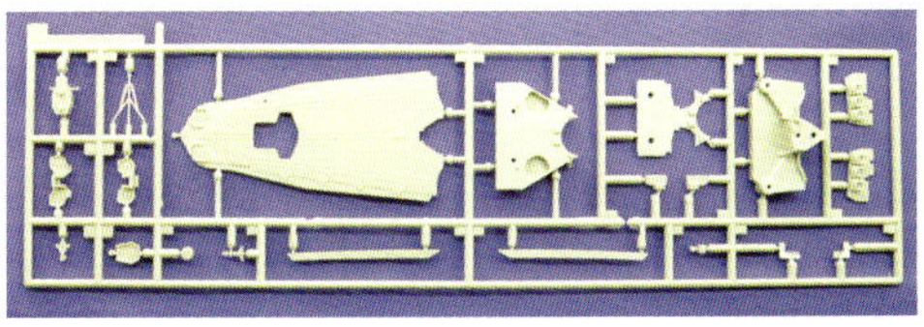

Left: Sprue with the flight deck parts

FUJIMI *ISE* CARRIER-BATTLESHIP

1:700 Scale

This kit is of *Ise* as she appeared during the Battle of Leyte Gulf in October 1944. It is an impressive kit; the box is loaded with parts.

The hull sides are moulded as one piece; the forecastle and quarterdeck are also a single large piece. The main armament has individual gun barrels; the two-piece funnel has a separate see-through grille; the searchlight platform supports and the catapults are solid pieces with well-defined lattice supports. Detailing is very good: wood decks have individual planks and raised bollards, capstans, anchor chain, hatches, and boat chocks where appropriate; metal decks have a non-skid pattern. Scuttles have rigols ('eyebrows'), the gun barrels have blast bags, pagoda and searchlight platforms have moulded-in supports underneath, and moulded-in bridge windows are on the applicable pagoda pieces.

The flight deck has moulded-in transport rails and turntables and the bomb hoist hatch is open; the hoist is moulded with a bomb attached. The elevator is a separate piece, but hangar details would need to be scratch-built if desired. The air group consists of 2 'Judy' and 2 'Paul' seaplanes, moulded in clear plastic. The searchlights are also moulded in clear plastic.

There are 380 parts on twenty-one sprues. The Japanese Navy Battleship Ordnance Set is not included, Fujimi electing to use their own highly detailed parts for the AA weapons and boats; some

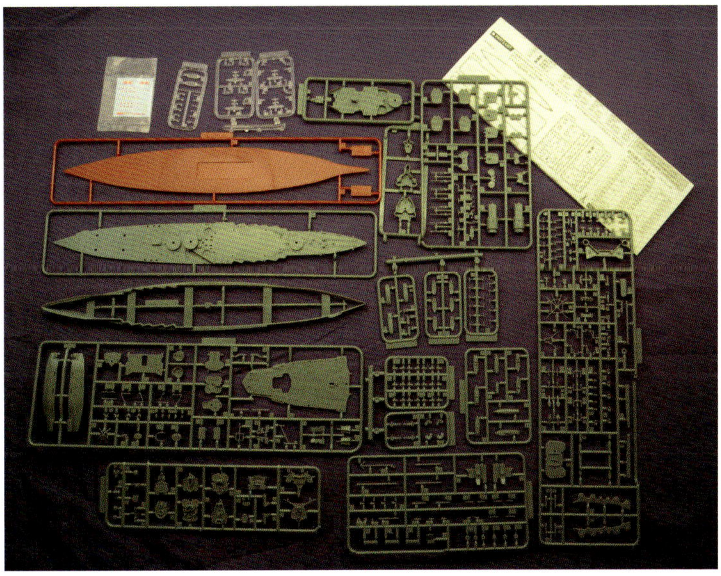

Above: Kit components

of the boats have oars across the thwarts. The instructions feature a comprehensive parts list and a profile drawing with painting instructions referencing the Mr Colour range. Decals for flags, ensigns, and aircraft markings are included.

The large part count and extensive detailing will certainly make this a very impressive model.

■ Review kit kindly lent by **imperialhobbies.ca**

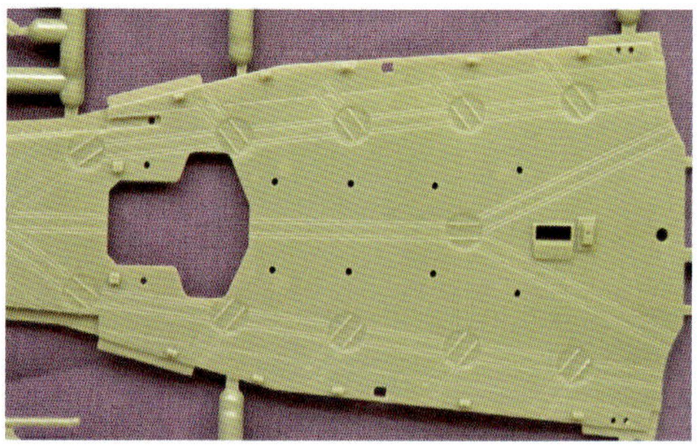

Right: Close-up of flight deck

FUJIMI *ISE* CARRIER-BATTLESHIP 1:350 Scale

Depicting *Ise* at Leyte Gulf, this is not just a simple scaling up of the 1:700 scale kit, far from it! With 1125 items on twenty-one sprues there are a lot of detail parts – the funnel is assembled from 9 pieces, each 5in AA gun from 6, the catapults from 7, and the aircraft trolleys have 5.

Below: The impressive number of parts included in the kit

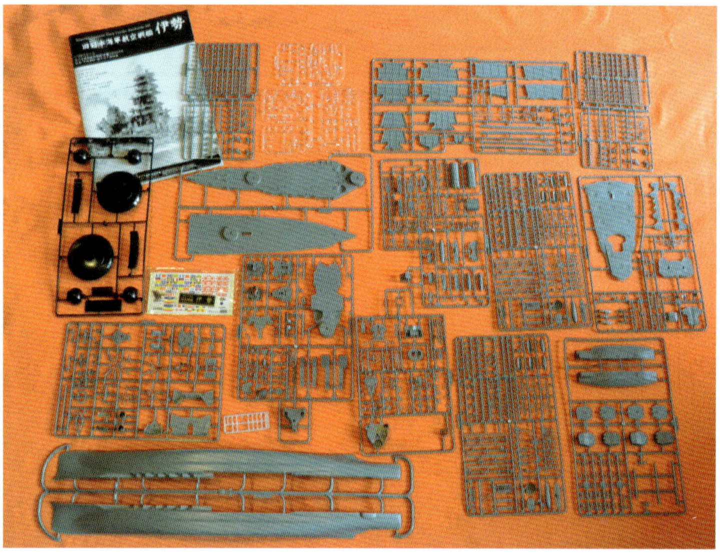

There is a very high level of detailing. The wooden decks have finely scribed individual planks, the metal decks have anti-skid patterns, bulkheads feature hatches and scuttles. The many deck fittings such as bollards, capstans, and hatches are individual parts instead of being moulded in. The detail parts are not just limited to the deck fittings; there are twelve lookout stations with binoculars on the top level of the bridge pagoda alone.

This is a full hull kit with the hull split into port and starboard halves. It features a degaussing cable, scuttles with rigols, the anti-torpedo bulge, and bilge keels. Fifteen internal supports are added during assembly to provide rigidity for the completed hull and support for the decks. The waterline is not marked requiring the use of the kit drawings to correctly place it. The aerial spreaders on the mainmast are very thin and all the lattice work is see-through and very delicate. Bridge windows are separate parts in clear plastic, as are the searchlights. The main armament blast bags are separate pieces and the gun barrels themselves feature drilled-out muzzles. The flight deck has very well defined transport rails set into the deck, with the bomb hoist open and the flight deck elevator a separate piece. The air group consists of 2 'Judy' and 2 'Paul' seaplanes, moulded in clear plastic. Anchor chain, a display stand, and decals for flags and aircraft markings are also included.

The instructions are in the form of a 20-page booklet, with a very large 31in x 21in full colour sheet featuring port, starboard, fore, aft, and overhead views in 1:350 and paint swatches from the Mr Colour range.

■ Review kit kindly lent by **Kerry Jang**

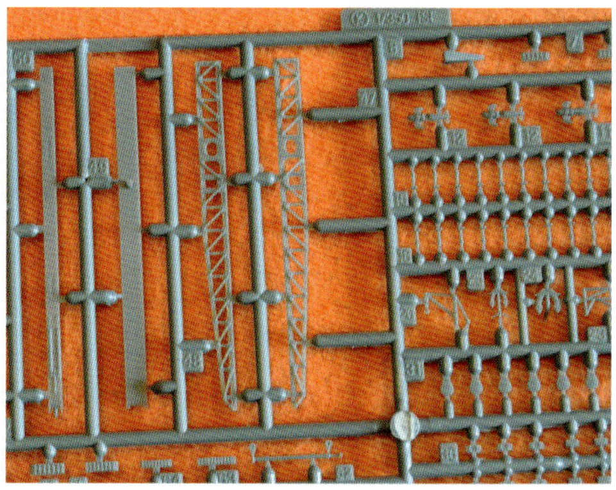

Right: Close-up of catapult

Photo-etch & Accessories

AOSHIMA *FUSO*/*YAMASHIRO* 1944 DETAIL SETS 1:700 Scale

These very comprehensive sets include a wooden deck and photo-etch sheet with over 200 parts. While specifically meant for the 1944 kit versions of the two ships, alternate parts are provided for the 1942 *Yamashiro*. Included are Type 13 and Type 21 radars, RDF loops, funnel grilles, crane boom and rigging, catapult, aircraft trolley, skidplates for anchor chains, anchor chain, pre-cut railings for turret tops and deck edges, hatch covers, cable reels, and ladders. The sets are not identical; the searchlight platforms are different for each ship and the *Yamashiro* set has a mainmast starfish and a degaussing cable, while *Fuso*'s has the correctly shaped conning tower platform and a mast for the PT Boat.

These are very high quality sets featuring plenty of relief etching, a double-sided full colour instruction sheet is included.

■ Review sets courtesy of **Aoshima Models**

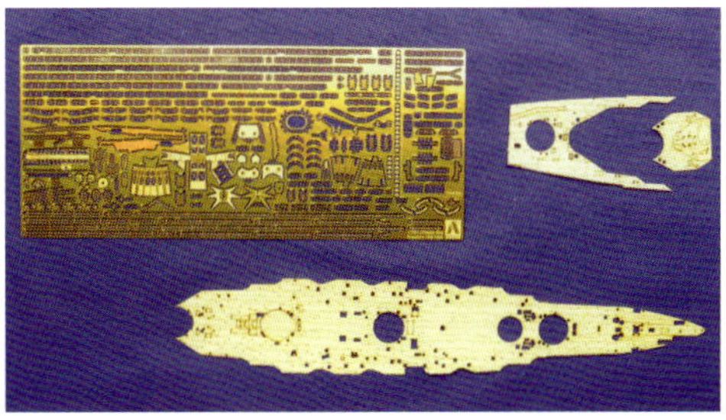

Left: Aoshima detail set for *Yamashiro* with etch sheet and wood deck

Below: Aoshima *Yamashiro* 1944 detail set

AOSHIMA *YAMASHIRO* 1944 ETCH SET 1:700 Scale

This set has a single steel photo-etch sheet with 106 parts for Type 21 radar, 36 single 25mm mounts with bases, funnel grille, davits, aircraft propellers, aircraft trolleys, small cranes, a catapult, crane boom, and searchlight towers. An easy set to use without a lot of complex parts, it comes with a double-sided instruction sheet.

ARTIST HOBBY *FUSO* 1941 DECK MASK 1:700 Scale

A relatively new accessory for ship modellers, deck masks feature low-tack masking tape pre-cut into sections that fit precisely over a kit model's decks while leaving deck detail such as hatches and capstans exposed for painting. They considerably ease the task of masking off the deck prior to painting the superstructure. This set has 22 pieces on one sheet for the Fujimi *Fuso* 1941 kit.

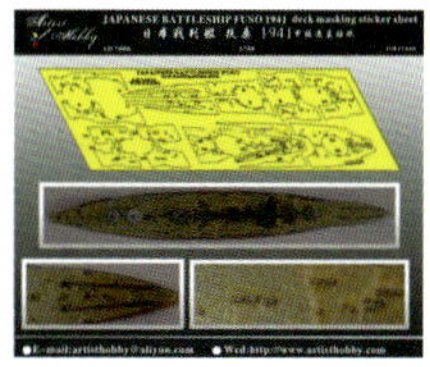

Above: Deck mask for Fujimi's *Fuso* 1941

FLYHAWK *FUSO* UPGRADE SET 1:350 Scale

Those wishing to fully outfit their Fujimi *Fuso* model will find almost everything they need in this extensive upgrade set, which features seventeen brass photo-etch sheets and machined brass 14in and 6in gun barrels. The 500+ parts include all the usual deck fittings, plus single, twin, and triple 25mm AA mounts, superstructure platforms, radar, mainmast starfish, aircraft deck, boat and aircraft fittings, as well as detailed bulkheads. Railings for the decks and turret tops are also included. The various replacement platforms have anti-skid decks and railings already attached.

There are three double-sided pages of instructions, featuring detailed drawings and photographs identifying each kit part, with precise folding instructions. A 5in AA gun upgrade kit is also included with its own photo-etch sheet, resin gun mounts, and machined brass gun barrels. When completed, each gun mount will consist of 7 resin and 29 photo-etch parts.

This is a very high quality set with considerable attention to detail and lots of relief etching, but most modellers will find it quite simple to use due to the large size of the components in this scale.

■ Review set courtesy of **Flyhawk Model**

Left: Two of the seventeen etch sheets, the 5in AA upgrade, and machined 14in barrels

PIT ROAD *YAMASHIRO* ETCH SET 1:700 Scale

This set is for the Hi-Mold *Yamashiro* kit and has 69 parts on a single steel photo-etch sheet: the aft bracing for the bridge pagoda, searchlight platforms, Type 21 and 13 radar, crane boom, RDF loops, AA gun bulwarks, aircraft trolleys, catapult, aircraft propellers, jack staff, ladders, and single 25mm guns. Easy to follow instructions are included.

■ Review set courtesy of **Kraken Hobbies**

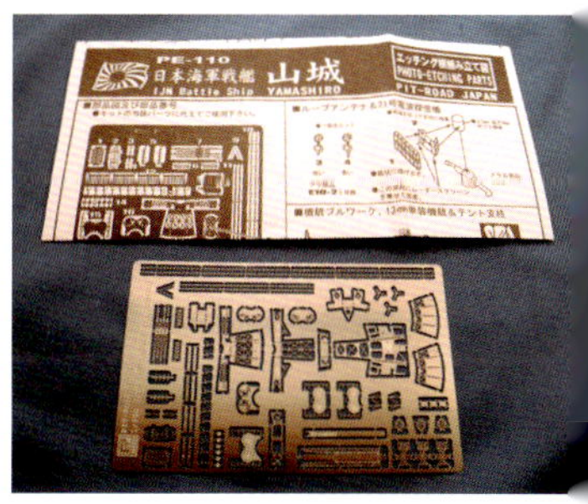

Above: Pit Road *Yamashiro* etch set and instruction sheet

FLYHAWK *FUSO*/*YAMASHIRO* DETAIL SETS 1:700 Scale

Designed for Aoshima kits, these comprehensive sets have four brass photo-etch sheets totalling more than 200 pieces. Besides the obvious details, pre-cut railing lengths for the decks and turret tops are also included. The sets are not

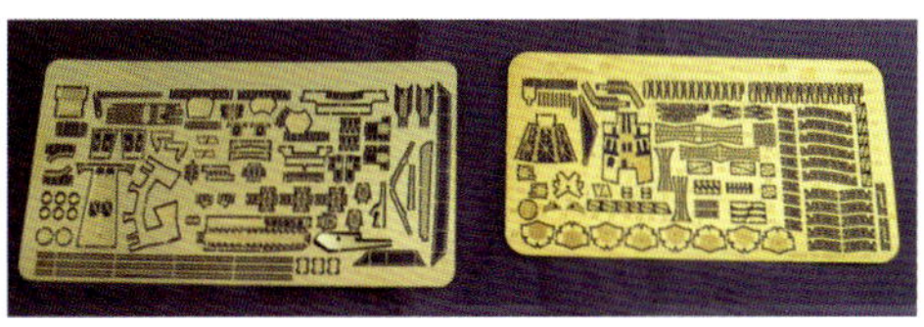

Left: Two of the four photo-etch sheets of the Flyhawk *Fuso* detail set

identical; the pieces for the bridge and searchlight platforms accurately reflect the differences between the two ships. Very high quality sets, they feature much relief etching and comprehensive instruction sheets.

■ Review sets courtesy of **Flyhawk Model**

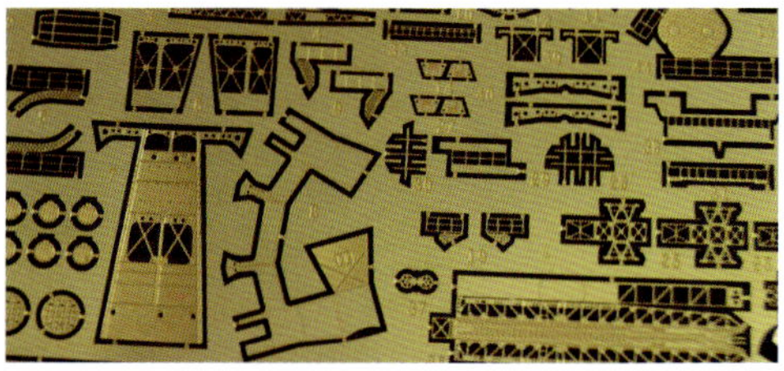

Right: Close-up of one of the *Fuso* photo-etch sheets, showing the level of fine detail and relief etching found throughout this set

FLYHAWK *YAMASHIRO* UPGRADE SET GOLD MEDAL EDITION

1:350 Scale

With wood decks and photo-etch, resin, and machined brass parts, this multi-media set of 600+ parts is packed with astonishing detail. Masts, yardarms, crane post, cable reels, capstans, boat booms, derrick boom, boat crane booms, mushroom vents, and 14in, 6in and 5in gun barrels are all from machined brass, over 300 parts in all. The resin parts include boats and canopies, air intakes, munitions lockers, winches, lookout stations with binoculars, 5in AA gun mounts, paravanes, and searchlights.

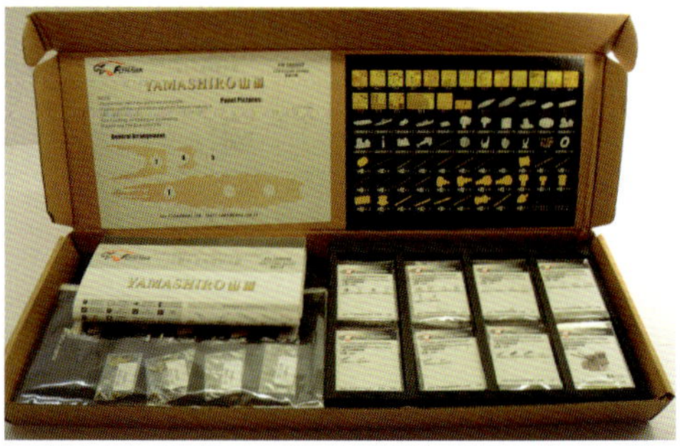

Right: Set components all neatly packed in boxes and sealed bags; wood decks are underneath

There are nineteen photo-etch sheets featuring extensive relief etching for ammunition lockers, superstructure platforms, funnel grilles, mainmast starfish, range clocks, twin 25mm AA mounts, catapult, aircraft deck, aircraft transport rails, crane boom and rigging, air intake grilles and a host of deck fittings and aircraft details.

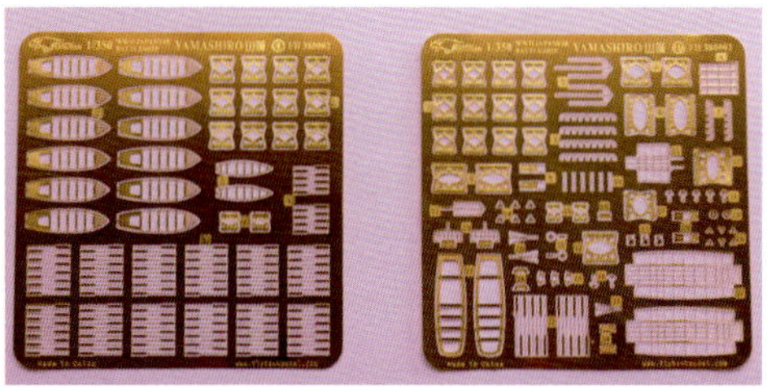

Right: Two of the nineteen photo-etch sheets, showing the fine detailing of this set

The wood deck consists of four pieces. Railings for the turret tops and the deck edges are also included and there are five double-sided pages of instructions with detailed drawings and photographs. The set is of exceptional quality, the resin parts being very well cast; the machined parts are nothing short of incredible, especially the capstans, vents, and cable reels.

■ Review set courtesy of **Flyhawk Model**

FUJIMI *FUSO* UPGRADE SET

1:350 Scale

There are four photo-etch sheets and eight machined brass barrels for the 5in AA guns in this set. Included in the 300+ parts are a catapult, crane boom and rigging, aircraft trolleys, life rings, hatches, air intake grilles, cable reels, Type 21 and 13 radar, derrick rigging, mainmast starfish, yardarms with ropes, cabins and rails for the boats, 25mm gun sights, shields, and bases, 14in gun details, searchlight platforms, pagoda bracing, funnel grille and baffles, ladders, and davits. The set also has pre-cut railing lengths for the deck and turret tops and two double-sided pages of instructions in full colour.

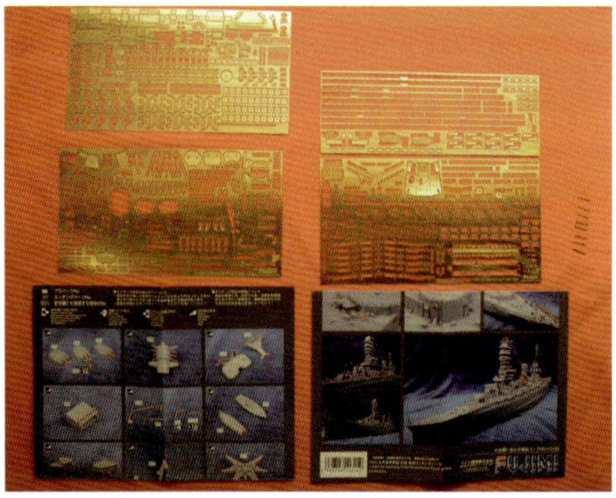

Right: The four sheets and eight barrels that make up this set, with the full colour instructions

■ Review set courtesy of **Kraken Hobbies**

RAINBOW MODEL *ISE* CLASS 1941/42 UPGRADE SET

1:700 Scale

This set is for the Hasegawa *Ise* class kits in their battleship configuration and features twelve photo-etch sheets from heavy quality brass, covered with protective plastic. Among the 400+ parts there are fittings for the main gun barrels; cabins, thwarts, and cradles for the boats; ready use ammunition lockers, funnel grilles, searchlight platforms, triple and twin 25mm mounts, details for the gun directors, aircraft struts, degaussing cable, bridge windows, pagoda platforms, Type 21 radar, replacement bulkheads, davits, aircraft deck catapult, crane boom, anchors, aircraft trolleys, turntables, cable reels, and ladders.

Twelve machined 14in gun barrels and the platform that replaced Hyuga's No 5 turret in May 1942 are also included. A very high quality set, it features plenty of relief etching and extensive instructions in full colour.

■ Review set courtesy of **Hobby Easy**

Left: Components of the set, twelve photo-etch sheets and machined 14in barrels

RAINBOW MODEL *ISE* CLASS 1944 UPGRADE SET

1:700 Scale

This very high quality set is for the Fujimi *Ise* class kits in their carrier-battleship configuration and features fifteen plastic-protected brass photo-etch sheets with over 500 pieces. Containing most of the superstructure and detail parts found in the 1941/42 set, it also features a flight deck built up in three layers with the elevator as a separate piece. Additional parts for the flight deck include supports and bracing, rocket launchers, catapults, turntables and transport rails, galleries for the 25mm and rocket launchers, single 25mm AA, canopies, struts, propellers, and wheels for the aircraft; AA platforms for the main turrets and eight machined 14in gun barrels are also included. There is no degaussing cable.

■ Review set courtesy of **Rainbow Model**

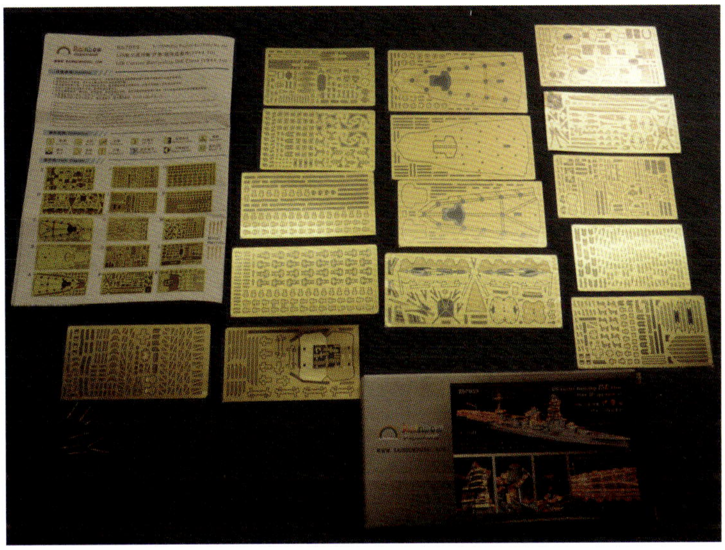

Below: The fifteen photo-etch sheets and machined 14in barrels that make up the set. Note the three-piece flight deck

LION ROAR *ISE* CLASS FLIGHT DECK

1:700 Scale

It has three plates that are sandwiched together to make up the flight deck with two of the plates being quite thick, which gives the completed deck plenty of 'heft'. The 'sandwich' construction allows the deck edge walkways to be slightly below the flight deck and the flight deck transport rails to protrude up through the deck.

There is a lot of etched relief. The transport rails and turntables are all separate pieces (totalling 103) and are all pre-cut; the instructions clearly label where each piece is to go. It can be used for any *Ise* or *Hyuga* carrier-battleship model as it is not kit-specific. There are no catapults or flight deck accessories included.

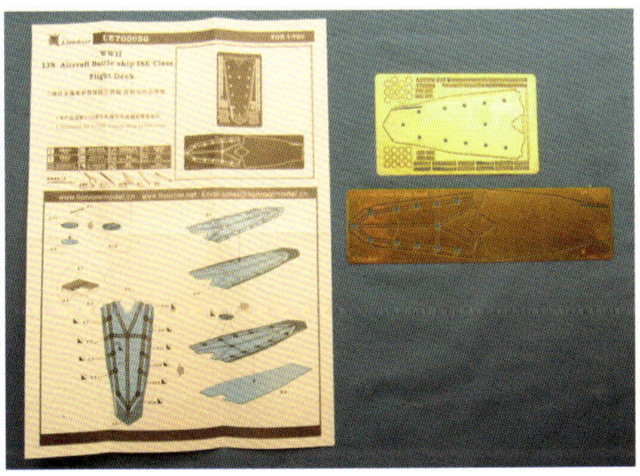

Left: Lion Roar flight deck showing the three large pieces that make up the deck

MASTER IJN 36cm/45 (14in) BRASS GUN BARRELS

1:700 Scale

Part of the Sea Master series, these machined gun barrels are finely tapered and feature hollowed out muzzles, hoops near the breech where the practice barrels were attached, and a pin to attach them to the gun mount. They are appropriate for all four ships. With ten barrels in the set, two sets will be required to outfit the battleships that have all twelve main guns.

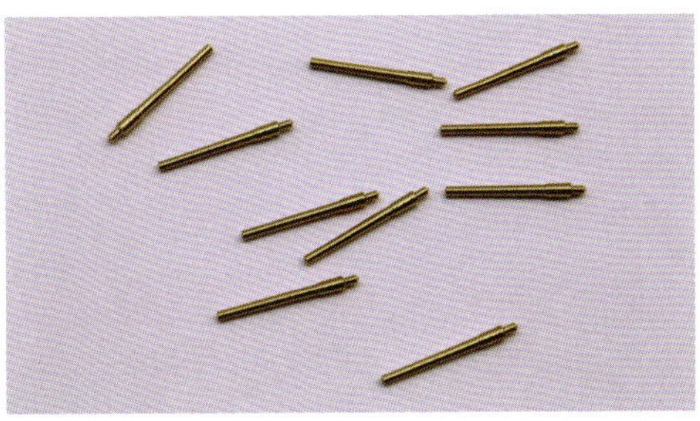

Left: The ten machined barrels in the Master IJN 14in gun set

GOLD MEDAL MODELS WW2 IJN BATTLESHIP ETCH SET

1:700 Scale

This set is for the original kits released prior to re-tooling with parts for all the Japanese battleships except for the *Yamato* class. Parts specifically for the *Fuso* and *Ise* classes are the searchlight towers, flight deck supports, and the catapult support for *Fuso*'s No 3 turret. The set also has a Type 21 radar array, catapults, aircraft propellers and trolleys, and deck railings. Enough pieces are supplied to outfit one ship. A very clear set of instructions is included.

Review photo courtesy **Gold Medal Models**

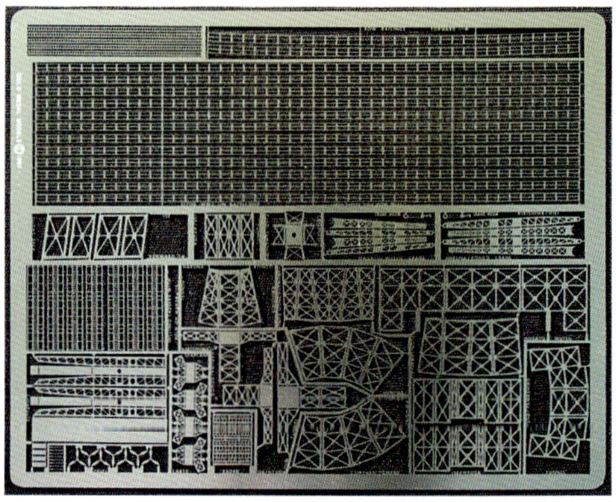

Right: GMM WW2 Japanese Battleship etch sheet

JAPANESE NAVY BATTLESHIP ORDNANCE SET

1:700 Scale

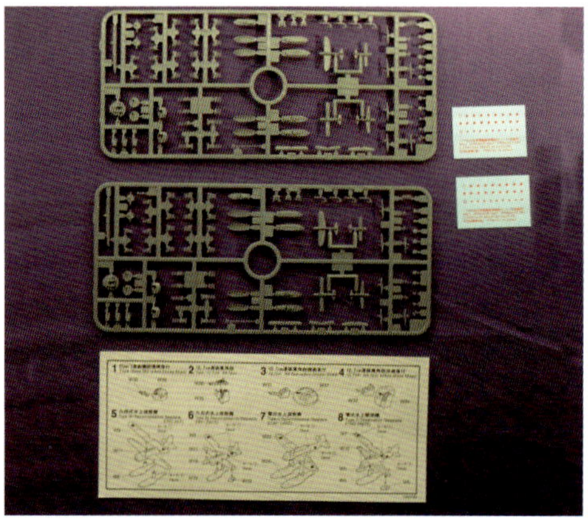

Right: The two sprues included with the Ordnance set

The ordnance sets are a clever innovation by the consortium of Japanese kit manufacturers to provide a standard set of detail parts for all their kits. Most re-tooled and new releases include one. Full of parts, they will provide ample spares once a project is completed.

There are several different sets – the battleship set consists of two sprues with 5in and 25mm AA guns, boats, searchlights, anchors, Type 13 and 22 radar, and four different aircraft: 'Alf', 'Dave', 'Jake', and 'Pete'.

ARTWOX *FUSO*/*ISE* WOOD DECKS

1:700 Scale

The Artwox deck for the Aoshima *Fuso* (Item AW20102) has two large pieces for the forecastle and quarterdecks, with two small pieces for the deck at the base of the pagoda. The deck for the Hasegawa *Ise* as fitted with the flight deck (Item AW20128) has six pieces for the forecastle, upper deck and the quarterdeck around No 3 and No 4 turrets; decks for nine ship's boats are also included.

Both decks come with anchor chain. The decks themselves are made from extremely thin wood, laser cut and featuring detailed deck planking with a peel and stick adhesive on the back. They are meant to fit over the existing kit decks with cut-outs for hatches and deck detail that should be removed with a sharp knife prior to fitting. A simple instruction sheet shows how the deck should appear when fitted.

Artwox produces decks for the Aoshima and Fujimi kits of *Fuso* and *Yamashiro*, the Fujimi *Ise* and both the battleship and carrier-battleship versions of the Hasegawa *Ise* and *Hyuga*.

Below: Artwox wood decks for *Ise* (top) and *Fuso* (bottom)

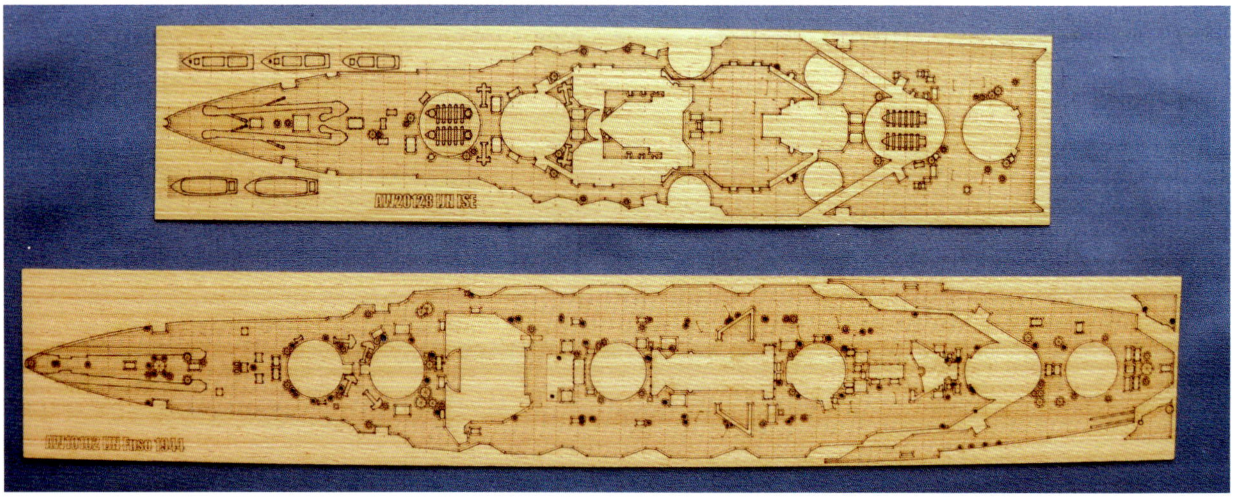

HUNTER *FUSO/YAMASHIRO/HYUGA* WOOD DECKS
1:700 Scale

These decks are for both versions of the Hasegawa *Hyuga* (Items W70018 & W70072), the Aoshima *Fuso* 1938 (Item W70087) and the Aoshima *Yamashiro* (Item W70006) and all feature four-piece decks. The *Fuso* deck extends all the way to the stern as it was not fitted with the aircraft handling deck on the quarterdeck in 1938. They are similar in characteristics to the Artwox product above.

Hunter also produces decks for the Aoshima 1944 *Fuso*, thc Fujimi 1944 *Fuso* and the battleship and carrier-battleship versions of the Hasegawa *Ise*; check for the appropriate deck for your project.

Review decks courtesy of **Flyhawk Model**

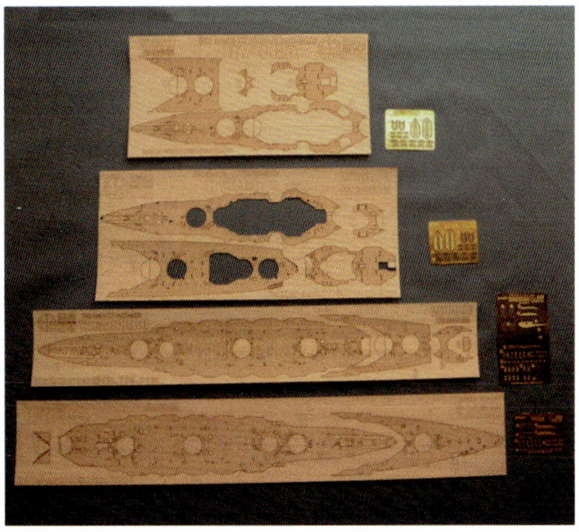

Left: Hunter decks (from the top) for *Hyuga* as a carrier-battleship, *Hyuga* as a battleship, *Yamashiro*, and *Fuso*

HUNTER *FUSO/ISE* WOOD DECKS
1:350 Scale

These decks are for the Fujimi kits of *Ise* (Item W35031) and *Fuso* (Item W35013). Both have four-piece decks for the main model and decks for the smaller boats. The included photo-etch sheet for *Ise* has small platforms and deck edge plates that were fitted abreast turret No 1. The sheet for *Fuso* includes bulwarks for the AA guns fitted to the main deck; both sheets have cable reels.

The sheets are very thin and feature finely detailed deck planking. Cut-outs for hatches and deck detail should be removed prior to fitting with a sharp knife; the peel-and-stick backing is used to attach the deck pieces to the model. Anchor chain and a simple instruction sheet are included.

Hunter also makes a deck for the Fujimi *Yamashiro*.

Review decks courtesy of **Flyhawk Model**

Below: Hunter deck for *Fuso* with the etch sheet

RAINBOW MODEL *ISE* CLASS DERRICK AND CRANE
1:350 Scale

This set is not kit-specific and includes two photo-etch sheets and three machined brass pieces featuring raised detail and tapered end caps. It will build into highly detailed and impressive assemblies; the derrick uses two of the machined brass pieces and 43 etch parts. The crane has six parts including a photo-etch boom and machined brass support post. Pulleys and hooks are supplied; the rigging is available separately from Rainbow Model. Easy to follow instructions are included.

Review sample courtesy of **Rainbow Model**

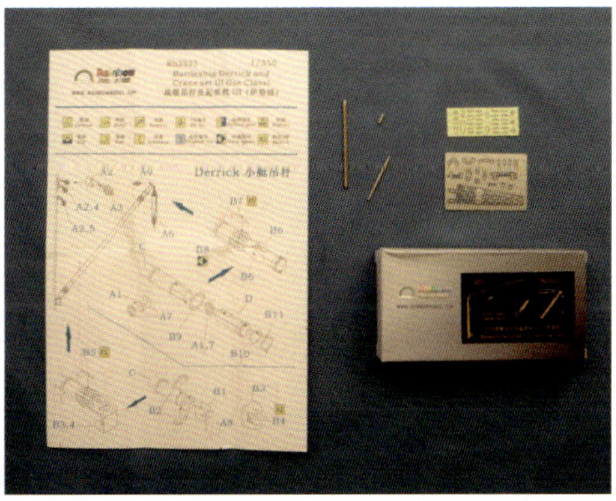

Left: Components of the set, note the three machined pieces for the crane and derrick posts

Below: Rainbow's set of cranes for every Japanese battleship, including all of the *Fuso* and *Ise* classes

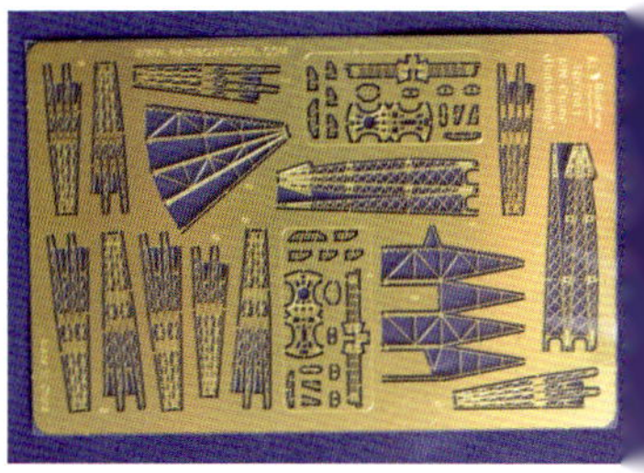

RAINBOW MODEL IJN BATTLESHIP CRANE ETCH SET
1:700 Scale

This single photo-etch sheet set has the crane booms for all the Japanese battleships of the Second World War, with enough being supplied to outfit all twelve of them. Featuring plenty of relief etching, it is not kit-specific. Modellers will need to supply hooks and rigging. Instructions are included.

Review sample courtesy of **Rainbow Model**

Modelmakers' Showcase

DIGITAL NAVY *FUSO* 1:250 scale

By JAN DOHMEN

Jan Dohmen writes:

I started card modelling after my retirement in 2004. I wanted to do something special with the Digital Navy model of *Fuso* and using a hi-res cross section drawing from Mr Gaspar Pina, a Spanish graphic designer, decided to build the model with the starboard mid-section and the lower part of the forward superstructure cut away. My short experience in the Royal Netherlands Navy helped me sort out the interior, even though modern ships are very different from the inside of a Japanese battleship. It took a lot of research and planning to get the details correct and I had to solve some difficulties in

making the model sturdy enough. It took me less than a year to complete, working from the inside out in small steps. Building in cross section is very different from a regular model. Not everything that is drawn in 3D is possible in physical model building, but there are many more challenges.

For rigging I used and still use the finest possible fishing wire from Gudebröd, and the figures are from Preiser.

FUJIMI ***FUSO*** 1:350 scale

By KOSTAS KATSEAS

Kostas Katseas writes:

The Fujimi kit is very nice; the bridge pagoda can be a small model by itself. In the diorama I wanted to show the influence a country's military architecture has on ship design – hence the inclusion of the mediaeval castle.

HI-MOLD *YAMASHIRO* 1:700 scale By LARS JUEL MOSBAEK

Lars Juel Mosbaek writes:

This is a very good model kit right from the box with no need for any improvements, but will be even better if one chooses to use photo-etch parts. To make the bridge windows I placed clear plastic behind horizontal ladders. The plating on the forward and aft hull sections was done with the help of masking tape. Some additional parts are from paper and wire, while the signal flags are hand-painted on household metal foil.

The building time was 7 weeks. For references I used the *Anatomy of the Ship Fuso* by Janusz Skulski, *Warships of the Imperial Japanese Navy* by Jentschura, Jung, and Mickel and *Japanese Warships of World War II* by A J Watts.

FUJIMI *FUSO* 1:700 scale

By KOSTAS KATSEAS

This remarkable diorama shows *Fuso* riding quietly at anchor alongside submarines *I-1* and *I-6*. The submarines are the Aoshima kits. *Fuso* is dressed up with details from Fine Molds; the figures are 3D printed.

AOSHIMA *YAMASHIRO* 1:700 scale

By LEO JAUDENES

The basic kit is a nice and simple build; Leo added etch parts from Flyhawk and AA guns from Fine Molds to add detail to his model, which represents *Yamashiro* ready to sail on her final sortie. He scratch-built the water barrels seen on deck, the hammocks and ropes used for splinter protection, and supports for the bridge pagoda. The auxiliary ship is also scratch-built.

The sea is made from Vallejo putty and the paints are Citadel acrylics. It was a long project, but very interesting.

FUJIMI *ISE* 1:350 scale

By ZDENĚK KRČMÁŘ

Zdeněk Krčmář writes:

The model depicts *Ise* during the Battle of Leyte Gulf in October 1944. The starboard catapult is trained outboard to clear the firing arcs for turret No 4.

For detailing, I used the Fujimi etch sets with some smaller parts like the ventilators coming from the Hasegawa *Nagato* kit. The wood deck is by MK1 Design; deck fittings, binoculars, voice pipes, and searchlights are from sets by Veteran Models. The gun barrels are from Master.

I used mainly Tamiya colours, gradually brightened with washes from MIG applied over top. All the antennas and rigging are from 0.06mm fishing line, coated with black matt Lifecolor paint after installation.

HASEGAWA *HYUGA* 1:700 scale

By LARS JUEL MOSBAEK

Lars Juel Mosbaek writes:

Hasegawa's new tooling is one of the best in the Japanese battleship range, but I found some things that needed attention. Before conversion, the top of *Hyuga*'s mainmast was T-shaped with red/green navigation lights above the starfish. *Ise* had the W-shaped mainmast and the navigation lights were under the starfish. After *Hyuga*'s conversion to carrier-battleship, her main-mast top was changed to the W-shape.

I first completed this ship in November 2005, scratch-building the searchlight platforms from styrene plastic, paper, and copper wire – my first plastic kit in 25 years! In 2007, with my skills much improved and with more references, I decided to rebuild it.

I disassembled the model down to the hull leaving only the funnel and main guns. The funnel lattice work was replaced with

surplus photo-etch from Tom's Modelworks. The entire aircraft deck was rebuilt with a new crane and the aircraft were painted in 1941 camouflage colours.

The windows on the pagoda tower are 1:350 ladders placed horizontally. The anchor chain is from a necklace and the anchors are white metal surplus from the Hi-Mold *Fuso/Yamashiro* kits. The boats are from Skywave, the hatches from Voyager, and the degaussing cable is from Lion Roar. I scratch-built a lot of details all over the ship, including the cable drums from copper wire and plastic

The hull was painted in Humbrol #7 Matt. I use a four-step process to paint wood decks using Vallejo paints. The first layer is sand coloured, the next is a mix of sand and white, then a mix of sand and brown, and finally just sand colour again. All the layers are applied by brush with each layer being randomly applied to different planks in order to give the final textured effect.

I added rigging and signal flags J, G, H, A for *Hyuga*. Rebuilding time was 2.5 weeks.

HASEGAWA *ISE* 1:700 scale

By JEFF LIN

Jeff Lin writes:

The Hasegawa kit is a sharp and clean 'platform' compared to the Fujimi new tooling *Ise*.

I built this kit in 2005 when there were not a lot of dedicated photo-etch sets available. I like to try various items to get the best match of materials for a project. The deck planking is made from strips of masking tape, 0.3mm wide and 20mm long. Rope is from copper wire; the anti-splinter protection and sandbags from putty. The bulwarks are made from aluminum sheet bought at a fishing supply shop.

Try not to limit your imagination even if you are using complete detail upgrade sets – build what you dream of.

FUJIMI *HYUGA* 1:350 scale

By KARL ZINGHEIM

Karl Zingheim writes:

The model is adapted from the Fujimi *Ise* kit and depicts *Hyuga* sunk at her moorings in July 1945, largely stripped of her AA armament. By carefully cutting a hole in the water base I was able to get the model to sit snugly without having to cut away the lower hull. I want to build the battleship version of this class, so I scratch-built the after two turrets to save the kit ones in the event that a full battleship kit is not released in 1:350.

The unusual mix of colours and hues on the wreck due to fire, rust, oil stains, and camouflage attracted the attention of US Navy Combat artist Standish Backus after the war when he painted several interesting scenes of both *Ise* and *Hyuga*. Reviewing colour footage of the 2010 oil spill in the Gulf of Mexico assisted my depiction of the oil slick in the diorama for which I used a mix of raw umber tube paint and flat black.

The initial application was allowed to partially dry then I worked on sections with a wet brush to thin some layers, giving the oil a sense of depth. The rest of the water base is brushed artist's gel over-painted with blue.

Hyuga **1941**

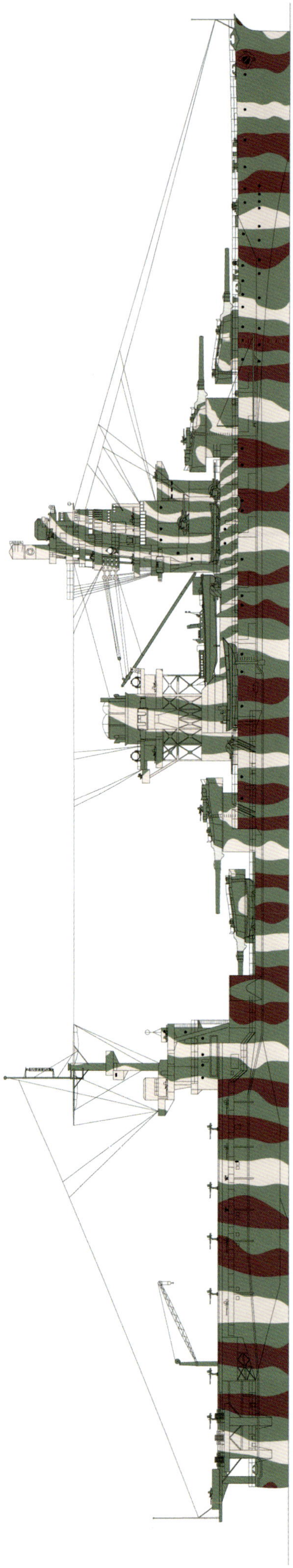

ISE **1945**

Appearance

PRE-RECONSTRUCTION ALTERATIONS

All four ships underwent constant modifications during the 1920s, the major ones being the rebuilding of the foremast, removal of the anti-torpedo nets and fitting a spoon-shaped cowl to the forward funnel.

RECONSTRUCTIONS

All four battleships were reconstructed in the 1930s. *Fuso* became the prototype for the IJN's 'Second Modification Plan' to be applied to the rest of the battle fleet. Subject to much experimentation, her reconstruction was extremely protracted, encompassing four phases over eleven years interspersed with in service periods to test the modifications.

***Fuso* First Phase – 12 April 1930 to 12 May 1933 at Kure.** The most extensive of the reconstruction phases, she emerged with new machinery, additional armour, anti-torpedo bulges, a catapult on the roof of No 3 turret, and increased elevation for the main and secondary guns. The AA fit was enhanced with the replacement of the 3in single guns by four twin 5in guns and four quad 13.2mm machine guns. The most noticeable changes were the removal of the forward funnel, the replacement of the mainmast with a large control tower, and the replacement of the foremast with a pagoda bridge that soared 144ft above the waterline. The combination of *Fuso*'s shortened bridge superstructure aft of turret No 2 and the repositioning of turret No 3 to

Above: Amidships detail of *Yamashiro* prior to reconstruction, offering a good view of the casemate guns. Turret No 4 has been fitted with a flying-off platform and the heavy derrick fitted to the mainmast can be seen. *(By courtesy of Ray Bean)*

PRE-RECONSTRUCTION ALTERATIONS

Fuso

1917. Main gun director fitted to the foretop

1918. Searchlights moved from the funnel to the lower part of the forward superstructure; 5 single 3in AA guns fitted

1919. Firing command platform fitted to the lower part of the forward superstructure

1920s. 3 single 6.5mm AA guns fitted

1922–3. 15ft rangefinders replaced with 26ft models; elevation of 14in guns increased

Jan 1924. Aircraft launch platform temporarily fitted to the roof of No 2 turret

1923–4. Foremast rebuilt

1925. Cowl added to forward funnel

1926. Torpedo net booms removed

1927–8. 6 single 3.1in AA guns fitted

Yamashiro

1917. Aircraft launch platform fitted to the roof of No 2 turret

1922. Aircraft launch platform removed

1923–4. Foremast rebuilt

1925. Cowl added to forward funnel

1927–8. Torpedo net booms removed; fore topmast removed, mainmast extended; searchlight platforms fitted around after funnel; 6 single 3.1in AA fitted

Ise

1921. Elevation of main guns increased to 30° extending the range to 30,400yds; 4 single 3.1in AA guns fitted

1926. Foretop enlarged with new rangefinders, range clocks, new charthouse and extra searchlight platforms

1927. Torpedo net booms removed; flying-off platform fitted to No 2 turret roof for a Mitsubishi 1MF3 Type 10 fighter

1928–9. Foremast rebuilt; cowl added to forward funnel; flying-off platform on No 2 turret removed; flying-off platform fitted to No 5 turret roof for a Yokosuka E1Y Type 14 floatplane

1930–1. Searchlight platforms fitted around after funnel; derrick for handling floatplanes installed at stern

20 Nov 1931 to 10 Feb 1932. 5.5in shielded guns on the forecastle removed; four twin 5in/40 AA shielded mounts fitted abreast the foremast; 2 twin 40mm fitted; mainmast top section shortened; flying-off platform and derrick removed; catapult and blister for crane engine installed on the stern

14 May to 5 Jun 1933. Collapsible aircraft crane fitted to the stern; 3 Nakajima E4N2 Type 90 floatplanes embarked

Hyuga

1921. Elevation of main guns increased to 30° extending the range to 30,400yds; 4 single 3.1in AA guns fitted

1926. Foretop enlarged with new rangefinders, range clocks, new charthouse and searchlight platforms

1927. Torpedo net booms removed; foremast rebuilt; cowl added to forward funnel; flying-off platform fitted to No 2 turret roof for a Mitsubishi 1MF3 Type 10 fighter

1928. Flying-off platform on No 2 turret removed; flying-off platform fitted to No 5 turret roof for a Yokosuka E1Y Type 14 floatplane

1930–1. Searchlight platforms fitted around after funnel; derrick for handling floatplanes installed at stern

1933. 5.5in shielded guns on the forecastle removed; four twin 5in/40 AA shielded mounts fitted abreast the foremast; 2 twin 40mm fitted; flying-off platform and derrick removed; collapsible aircraft crane, Kure Type 2 Catapult, and blister for crane engine installed on the stern; 3 Nakajima E4N2 Type 90 floatplanes embarked

point forward resulted in the base of her pagoda being shorter in length than the decks above, contributing to its startlingly unstable appearance.

An aircraft elevator was fitted on the port side of turret No 3, sitting above deck level as its lifting machinery was directly under it. Aircraft stored on deck were moved on their trolleys by block and tackle and winches up transport rails to the elevator which then lifted the trolley to the catapult. A 65ft derrick was fitted to the back of the pagoda on the port side for aircraft recovery. It was a very cumbersome system and was not fitted to *Yamashiro*. Three floatplanes were assigned to the ship, two stowed on trolleys on the forecastle deck and one on the catapult.

***Fuso* Second Phase – 16 September 1934 to 19 February 1935 at Kure.** The anti-torpedo bulges were enlarged and raised to the top of the hull, a motor room for a crane was fitted to the port side of the quarterdeck, the forward searchlight platform on the funnel was lowered to provide more space for handling aircraft, and the stern was lengthened by 25ft. The combination of the upgraded machinery and the greater hull length increased her speed to 24.75 knots.

***Fuso* Third Phase – 26 February 1937 to 31 March 1938 at Kure.** It was found that the increase in speed and increase in draught caused the forward casemate guns to be washed out when steaming at high speeds so this phase saw the removal of the forward 6in casemate gun on each side. The four quad 13.2mm guns were replaced with eight twin 25mm guns.

***Fuso* Fourth Phase – 19 December 1940 to April 1941 at Kure.** The top two levels of the pagoda were removed and replaced with an air defence station, lowering the pagoda height by 7ft. The catapult was removed from No 3 turret along with the elevator and derrick. A catapult, transport rails, turntables, crane, and linoleum-covered aircraft deck were all fitted on the quarterdeck.

Below: *Fuso* in the final stages of her first reconstruction, 28 April 1933 at Kure. The great beam below the waterline as a result of the torpedo bulges is evident. The ship is a beehive of activity; the scaffolding is very rudimentary considering that the workers are at least 30 feet above the dock floor. *(By courtesy of Ray Bean)*

FUSO CLASS RECONSTRUCTION DETAILS

Machinery

6 oil-fired boilers replaced the original 24 mix-fired boilers

75,000shp turbines replaced the original engines, doubling the power

Protection

¾in high tensile steel placed over the original hull plating outboard of the machinery spaces

Armour over the machinery and magazines increased to 5.1in

Armour around the lower funnel uptakes increased to 7in

Armoured deck increased between 2in and 3.8in

Main turret barbette armour increased

Anti-torpedo bulges added

Weight of the increased armour protection is 12,199 tons, a 42 per cent increase. Horizontal protection is high-tensile steel

Armament

Forward 6in casemate gun on both sides removed

3.1in AA guns removed

Torpedo tubes removed

The recoil and loading systems for the main armament changed from hydraulic power to compressed air, eliminating the problems with the firing cycles and enabling full broadsides to be fired

Elevation of the 14in main armament increased to 43°, extending range to 38,700yds

Elevation of the 6in guns increased to 30°

Four twin 5in/40 AA shielded mounts fitted abreast the bridge and on the aft control tower

Light AA changed to: 8 twin 25mm

Superstructure

Foremast replaced with a 144ft high pagoda structure consisting of 14 levels

Stern lengthened by 25ft

Fore funnel removed

Mainmast replaced with a massive control tower

Sternwalk removed from *Yamashiro*

32ft rangefinder fitted atop the pagoda

Platforms for 6 searchlights built around the funnel.

Aircraft

A 64ft catapult, rails and turntables, crane, and linoleum-covered aircraft deck fitted on the quarterdeck

3 Nakajima E4N2 Type 90 floatplanes embarked

ISE CLASS RECONSTRUCTION DETAILS

Machinery

8 oil-fired boilers replaced the original 24 mix-fired boilers

80,000shp turbines replaced the original engines, doubling the power

Protection

1in Type D steel fitted amidships on the outside of the hull from the forecastle deck to the turn of the bilge

Armour thickness over the machinery spaces and magazines increased to 4.7in

1in and 1¼in layers added to the main armoured deck

The deck abutting the top of the side belt was given 2¼in armour

Sloping sides of the deck armour increased by 1¼in

Anti-torpedo bulges fitted

Armour weight rose from 9500 tons to 12,100 tons. Horizontal protection is high-tensile steel

Armament

2 foremost casemate mounts removed

3.1in AA guns removed

40mm and 13.2mm AA guns removed

Torpedo tubes removed

Elevation of the 14in main armament increased to 43° for Nos 1, 2, 3, 4, and 5 turrets, extending range to 38,700yds

Elevation for No 6 increased to only 33° as the barbette lacked the necessary depth

Elevation of the 5.5in guns increased to 30°, extending range to 20,800yds

Light AA changed to: 10 twin 25mm

Superstructure

Foremast replaced with a 135ft high pagoda structure

Stern lengthened by 25ft

Fore funnel removed

Mainmast replaced with a small control tower

32ft rangefinder fitted atop the pagoda

Aircraft

Catapult replaced by a Kure Type No 2 Mod 5 model

Transport rails and turntables fitted at the stern

3 Nakajima E8N1 Type 95 ('Dave') floatplanes embarked

Fuso underwent stability trials on 20 April 1941 where she was inclined to 8.1° via use of the counter-flooding system. Despite there being no official concerns with her stability, the crew was very nervous, feeling that after the list reached 4° that she would not return to normal if it was increased further.

***Yamashiro* – 18 December 1930 to 30 March 1935 at Yokosuka.** *Yamashiro* was fitted with all of *Fuso*'s internal and external upgrades, with a few differences. Turret No 3 remained facing aft when stowed, allowing the pagoda bridge to extend further aft than *Fuso*. The pagoda bridge also featured much heavier bracing on the rear. Her initial AA fit was four twin 5in guns, two twin 40mm, and two quad 13.2mm machine guns. She carried her full outfit of sixteen 6in guns until March 1938 when the forward pair was removed. The 40mm and 13.2mm were replaced at that time with eight twin 25mm.

Despite the effort and money spent, the reconstruction of the two ships was seen as only a limited success due to the amount of experimentation with the bridgework. Many considered the upgrades to be of no real benefit as the ships were too old, with some of the opinion that the ships were 'useless, obsolete, and beyond rejuvenation'. After modernisation, *Fuso* was described as the ugliest ship in the Imperial Navy.

***Ise* – 01 August 1935 to 23 March 1937 at Kure; *Hyuga* – 23 November 1934 to 07 September 1936 at Kure.** Drawing on the experience gained with the *Fuso* and *Yamashiro*, their reconstructions were

Above: *Fuso* undergoing post-reconstruction trials, 10 May 1933. The catapult and derrick on the rear of the pagoda can be clearly seen. The blast problem for the secondary armament is readily evident as all the gun mounts are directly under the muzzles of the four forward turrets. The bulges are not yet extended to the top of the hull and the stern has not been lengthened. *(Author's collection)*

SUMMARY OF CHARACTERISTICS AS RE-BUILT

	Fuso Class	*Ise* Class
Displacement (Full Load)	39,154	40,169
Dimensions	Length 698ft, Beam 108ft 6in, Draught 31ft 9in	Length 708ft, Beam 104ft 1in , Draught 30ft 2in
Armament	12 – 14in/45, 14 – 6in/50, 8 – 5.0in/50, 16 – 25mm	12 – 14in/45, 16 – 5.5in/50, 8 – 5in/50, 20 – 25mm
Armour (maximum thickness)	Belt: 12in, Deck: 5.1in, Barbettes: 12in Turrets: 12in face, 8in sides, 4.5in roof CT: 13.75in	Belt: 12in, Deck: 4.7in, Barbettes: 12in Turrets: 12in face, 8in sides, 4.5in roof CT: 12in
Machinery	4 steam turbines @75,000shp 6 oil-fired boilers	4 steam turbines @80,825shp 8 oil-fired boilers
Range	11,800nm @ 16 knots	7780nm @ 16 knots
Top Speed	24.75 knots	25.3 knots

much quicker despite involving much the same scale of work. They both emerged with a radically altered profile, featuring the massive pagoda structure and single funnel with the aircraft handling arrangements located at the stern.

CARRIER-BATTLESHIP CONVERSION

The Japanese Navy initiated a massive carrier construction program after the loss of four aircraft carriers at Midway in June 1942, but none of the new carriers would be ready until 1944. To bridge the gap, a number of conversion projects were initiated that could be completed by mid-1943. Chief among these was the conversion of the *Ise* class to aircraft carriers. The slow battleships had been difficult to fit into the new tactical reality after December 1941 when the fast carriers came to dominate naval operations. Converting them to carry their own air groups would transform them into potentially valuable fleet units.

Several different proposals were studied including conversions to full carriers by removing all the main gun turrets and fitting a 690ft flight deck, but the simplest proposal was to fit a flight deck in place of the two aftermost turrets and use catapults to launch the air group. In terms of time and material this was the most effective solution and was the option finally chosen. Plans were drawn up by the end of August 1942. At first *Fuso* and *Yamashiro* were considered for conversion, but the *Ise* class were chosen instead as their after turret could only elevate to 33° and *Hyuga* was already without turret No 5 after the explosion in May 1942.

Both ships were converted in 1943: *Ise* at Kure from 23 February to 5 September, and *Hyuga* at Sasebo from 2 May to 30

Below: *Fuso* after the second phase of her reconstruction in 1935. The hull has been lengthened and the characteristic 'V' shaped stern can be seen. The rangefinder at the top of the pagoda is the 26ft version. An aircraft is visible on the catapult. *(By courtesy of Ray Bean)*

Above: *Yamashiro* 6 months away from completion of reconstruction on 20 October 1934. Note the heavy bracing on the back of the pagoda and under the 5in gun tubs on the after control position. *(By courtesy of Ray Bean)*

November. Part of the equipment for *Hyuga* was built at Kure when *Ise* was converted, so her conversion was much quicker.

Conversion details. The turrets, barbettes, and roller paths of turrets No 5 and No 6 were removed along with all the casemate guns and their armour.

In place of the turrets a large hangar topped with a flight deck was constructed extending from the after control tower to the stern. Making use of material from the cancelled fourth *Yamato* class battleship, the hangar was 19ft high and 130ft long, of all-welded construction with considerable stern and side overhangs. The after control tower provided air crew space, stores and maintenance and repair shops. There was a transport rail on each side along which the aircraft were moved on trolleys and then clamped down for stowage. Four aircraft were carried on each rail, with one more stowed aft ahead of the lift.

The hangar was connected to the flight deck by a hydraulically operated lift fitted at the after end of the hangar. It was 'T' shaped and fitted with a transport rail that mated with the rails on the flight deck and on the hangar deck.

The flight deck was 230ft long. There were three longitudinal transport rails, one to port, one to starboard and one in the centre, connected by turntables on the centre rail at the aft and forward ends. The port and starboard rails had five turntables each for stowage of aircraft, with an additional aircraft stowed on the aft centreline turntable. The deck was topped with 8in of concrete to help compensate for the weight of the removed turrets. Despite the size of the flight deck, it was not of sufficient

Left: A close-up of *Fuso*'s bridge as it was at the beginning of 1935. Note the two directors fitted atop the conning tower. *(Author's collection)*

Above: *Fuso* conducting a flooding and pumping test at Kure, 20 April 1941. The 32ft rangefinder can be seen atop the pagoda and the catapult has been removed from turret No 3. Note the extension on the port side aft for the aircraft crane motor room and that turret No 6 does not carry a rangefinder. The three Nakajima E4N2 Type 90 aircraft are sporting camouflage schemes. *(By courtesy of Ray Bean)*

CHARACTERISTICS AFTER 1943 CONVERSION

Displacement (Full Load)	38,676 tons
Dimensions	Length 721ft, Beam 104ft 1in, Draught 29ft 8in
Armament	8 – 14in/45, 16 – 5in/50, 57 – 25mm
Range	9500nm @ 16 knots. Other characteristics unchanged

length to allow for take-offs or landings. Two 82ft catapults were installed at its forward end for launching the aircraft.

The rail system made it easy to move the aircraft around in a methodical manner. Aircraft moved up on the elevator to the after turntable on the flight deck, which was used to put them on the correct outside rail where they then moved to the catapults. The centre rail was used to return the trolleys. This was the same system used on the *Chitose* class seaplane tenders. The collapsible derrick previously on the quarterdeck was fitted to the port side of the flight deck for recovering floatplanes. A total of 22 aircraft could be carried: 2 on the catapults, 11 on the flight deck, and 9 in the hangar with the planned aircraft being the Yokosuka D4Y Suisei ('Judy') dive bomber.

Many safety measures learned from the disaster at Midway were incorporated. Foam and CO^2 firefighting systems were installed, and the hangar was fully enclosed and made airtight to prevent fumes from penetrating adjacent compartments. Gasoline filling points were fitted on the flight deck along with an armoured bomb hoist so all fueling and arming of aircraft took place on the flight deck. Bombs and munitions were stowed in turret No 5's magazine with avgas and oil stores in No 6's magazine.

The protection for the steering gear was also upgraded. An auxiliary steering room was fitted at the lower deck level of turret No 5, equipped with diesel-driven pumps but also capable of manual operation. This new compartment and the main steering room were surrounded by 3ft of poured concrete and fitted with a 6in thick armoured cover made from the removed turret armour.

The anti-aircraft armament was increased considerably, four additional twin 5in mounts being added on the forecastle and shelter decks. The existing ten twin 25mm mounts were replaced with nineteen triple 25mm mounts. The Type 21 radar was upgraded, and Type 22 and Type 13 sets fitted. Two 46ft Daihatsu landing barges were substituted for some boats.

Events quickly overtook the program and revealed the muddled thinking behind the concept. Accepting a short flight deck ruled out any possibility of the ships carrying their own CAP fighters. The additional 44 'Judy's carried aboard the two ships would have been a welcome addition to any air strike, but they would have had to recover aboard accompanying regular carriers. The ships carried enough bombs and fuel for three strikes but there was no

WARTIME ALTERATIONS

Other than the conversion of *Ise* and *Hyuga* to carrier-battleships, wartime alterations were limited to upgrades of the light AA armament and the installation of radar.

Fuso

18 Jul 1943 to 24 Jul 1943. Type 21 radar fitted to the front of the main rangefinder; light AA changed to: 17 single 25mm, 10 twin

2 Aug 1944 to 14 Aug 1944. 2 forward searchlights on funnel removed; side scuttles under the upper deck blanked off; platform over CT reduced in size to clear AA mounts on No 2 turret; 2 Type 13 radar sets fitted to the funnel; 2 Type 22 radar sets fitted to the air defence platform; Infra-red IFF gear installed; light AA changed to: 39 single 25mm, 16 twin 25mm, 8 triple 25mm, 10 single 13.2mm

Yamashiro

July 1943. Type 21 radar fitted to the front of the main rangefinder; light AA changed to: 17 single 25mm, 10 twin

20 Jul 1944 to 10 Aug 1944. Air defence centre fitted one level below the top of the pagoda; side scuttles under the upper deck blanked off; 2 Type 13 radar sets fitted to the mainmast; 2 Type 22 radar sets fitted to the air defence platform

Infra-red IFF gear installed; 6 Daihatsu landing barges carried; light AA changed to: 34 single 25mm, 17 twin 25mm, 8 triple 25mm, 10 single 13.2mm, 3 twin 13.2mm

Ise

25 May 1942 to 29 May 1942. Engine room repairs due to flooding casualty on 11 May; one of the first experimental Type 21 radar sets is fitted

23 Feb 1943 to 5 Sep 1943. Conversion to carrier-battleship. Light AA changed to: 19 triple 25mm

24 May 1944 to 31 May 1944. Sponsons added to flight deck for additional triple 25mm mounts; Type 22 radar replaced with improved sets; infra-red IFF gear installed; light AA changed to: 11 single 25mm, 31 triple 25mm

22 Jul 1944 to 26 Jul 1944. One E27 radar detector installed

18 Sep 1944 to 10 Oct 1944. Sponsons added to flight deck for rocket launchers; light AA changed to: 11 single 25mm, 31 triple 25mm, 6 30-barrelled 4.7in rocket launchers

29 Oct 1944 to 8 Nov 1944. Catapults removed

Hyuga

6 May 1942 to 25 May 1942. Turret No 5 removed and replaced with a circular armoured plate for 4 triple 25mm mounts; Type 22 radar prototype is embarked for tests; light AA changed to: 10 twin 25mm, 4 triple 25mm

2 May 1943 to 30 Nov 1943. Conversion to carrier-battleship; light AA changed to: 19 triple 25mm

May 1944. Sponsons added to flight deck for additional triple 25mm mounts; light AA changed to: 11 single 25mm, 31 triple 25mm

Jun 1944. Type 22 radar replaced with improved sets; infra-red IFF gear installed; one E27 radar detector installed

Sep 1944. Sponsons added to flight deck for rocket launchers; light AA changed to: 11 single 25mm, 31 triple 25mm, 6 30-barrelled 4.7in rocket launchers

7 Nov 1944. Catapults removed

way to bring aircraft back aboard to re-arm.

The standard 'Judy' was not strong enough to be catapulted so airframe modifications were required. The prototype was not ready until March 1944 and suffered many teething problems, so a mixed air group of 11 'Judy' and 11 Aichi E16A1 ('Paul') reconnaissance seaplane bombers was substituted instead. The 'Paul's could have been recovered, but having only one crane for 11 aircraft would have meant a very long recovery cycle and involved considerable difficulty as the crane was over 25ft feet above the waterline. During battle, the battleships would not have been able to stop to recover any of them. Moreover, the large size and position of the catapults interfered with the training arcs of No 4 turret.

Given time, solutions could no doubt have been found for these issues but time was something that Japan did not possess. In retrospect, the resources would have been more effectively used to build ASW ships.

Anti-aircraft weapons. All four ships were fitted with single 3in/40 Type 3 AA guns during the 1920s. As aircraft became larger and faster, the guns rapidly became outmoded and were replaced during reconstruction with twin 5in/40 Type 89 guns. This dual purpose gun was hampered by a

Left: *Hyuga* in 1935 after reconstruction. The large derrick fitted to the rear of the bridge pagoda for handling the ship's boats can be seen. Note that the 25mm AA have yet to be fitted to the funnel area. *(By courtesy of Ray Bean)*

Right: Rear view of *Ise*'s reconstructed pagoda. This is likely a pre-war photo as the Type 21 radar mattress has not been fitted and the director is not painted white. The pulleys and cables for the boat derrick can be seen to the left with the 32ft rangefinder at the top. *(US Navy)*

barrage fire doctrine which assumed that attacking aircraft would maintain a steady altitude and heading. This made it very difficult to hit anything. It is interesting to note that two of the mountings on *Fuso* and *Yamashiro* had to be positioned high on the aft control tower as there was no available deck space that would not be affected by blast from the 14in guns.

Light AA was provided by the 13.2mm and 25mm guns. The 13.2mm projectile was too light to seriously damage an attacking aircraft. The 25mm gun mount was too slow in train and elevation, gun sights could not handle fast targets, the gun had excessive vibration and muzzle blast and the magazine was too small.

The rocket launchers fitted to *Ise* and *Hyuga* in 1944 fired time-fused rockets armed with phosphorous incendiary charges and shrapnel. The launching crews had to wear special protective suits and stand behind shielding prior to launch. Likely more of a hazard to their crews than attacking aircraft due to the rocket motors and phosphorous charges, they were markedly ineffective.

AA shells were developed for the 14in, but also proved ineffective, if somewhat spectacular. The lack of a proximity fuse also hurt AA results. Very few aircraft were brought down attacking Japanese battleships.

AA ARMAMENT CHARACTERISTICS

Weapon	Maximum Elevation	Horizontal Range (yards)	Vertical Range (feet)	Rate of Fire (rpm)	Shell Weight (pounds)
3in/40 Type 3	75°	11,800	23,000	13	13
5in/40 Type 89	90°	16,100	31,000	8	51
13.2mm Type 93	85°	7100	14,700	450	1
25mm Type 96	80°	8200	17,200	220	1.8
4.7in Rocket	80°	4600	7500	16	49

RADAR CHARACTERISTICS

Type	Physical Appearance	Detection Range
Type 13 Air Search	Ladder	Aircraft group 100km Single aircraft 50km
Type 21 Air Search	Mattress	Aircraft group 100km Single Aircraft 70km
Type 22 Surface Search	Two horns, upper for reception lower for transmission	Battleships 35km Cruisers 20km Destroyers 17km

Sensors. Despite lagging well behind the Allies in the development of radar technology, the Imperial Navy still managed to produce three operational sets by 1944. They suffered from problems with background 'clutter' and the detection ranges given were obtained under optimal conditions, but they were effective nonetheless. *Yamashiro* made good use of her Type 22 when engaging the Allied cruiser line at Surigao Strait.

The prototype Type 21 set was tested aboard *Ise* during May 1942 at the same time as the prototype Type 22 was being tested aboard *Hyuga*. Both sets were successfully used for detection and for navigation, but *Hyuga*'s captain had her Type 22 removed as he deemed it unsatisfactory.

All four ships were also fitted with infrared IFF gear in 1944, featuring infra-red transmitting and receiving lamps. A pair of binoculars mounted with the transmitting lamp allowed ships to use the system for rudimentary signalling or as a formation light for station-keeping at night.

Camouflage and markings. The four ships did not carry any camouflage scheme while operational. They were painted in the standard dark grey on the hull, along with the metal decks, gun turrets, fittings, boat's sides and cabins, and the decks of the open boats. This was made from a mix of 75 per cent white, 15 per cent black, 6 per cent brown, and 4 per cent blue, a shade very similar to the current colour of the JMSDF. During the war paint stocks became short and the colour become more silver-grey. Each major depot unintentionally used a slightly different shade of grey: Maizuru was the lightest, with Kure, Yokosuka, and Sasebo each being progressively darker.

The underwater hull was painted reddish-brown made from a mix of 65 per cent brown, 20 per cent red, 10 per cent black, and 5 per cent white. This colour was also used to paint the underwater hull of the 56ft steam pinnace from 1915 to 1930. The decks were unpainted teak which would weather to grey-tan. The inside surfaces of the boats, the decks of the motor boats, and gratings were left in natural wood.

Funnel tops and fore and aft topmasts and any target barge carried were black semi-gloss. The bow mounted chrysanthemum was gold as were the characters for the ship's name carried on the side near the stern. The aircraft handling decks were covered in 2m wide linoleum sheets coloured dark yellowish brown (a pale milk chocolate colour), held down by 30mm wide brass strips. During the war, the rangefinders atop the bridge were painted white as a recognition feature, along with small stripes on the rear mast and any inscriptions on the boats. White canvas was used in peacetime as windscreens, blast bags, and cable reel and searchlight covers. Light brown or grey canvas was used during the war.

Ise's camouflage scheme in 1945 is a matter of conjecture: some sources indicate overall olive green, with dark green, yellow, grey, and red-brown splotches while others note the scheme shown on page 48. *Hyuga* remained dark grey, with dark green curves painted on her turrets.

Grey, black, and white were all semi-gloss.

Visual differences. The two classes could be easily distinguished from each other by the layout of the amidships turrets. *Fuso* and *Yamashiro* had theirs separated by the after funnel, *Ise* and *Hyuga's* were grouped together behind the after funnel.

There were a number of differences between *Fuso* and *Yamashiro* that make it relatively easy to tell them apart. During her entire service career, the forward superstructure on *Yamashiro* extended to the base of No 2 barbette; on *Fuso* there was a gap between the forward superstructure and No 2 barbette. *Yamashiro* carried a sternwalk from completion until her major reconstruction; *Fuso* did not have one. From completion until modernisation *Yamashiro* sported a single rangefinder on the top of the conning tower; *Fuso* had two fitted there. From 1927 *Yamashiro* had a searchlight platform on the front of the after funnel that was not fitted to *Fuso*.

Above: Close-up of *Ise*'s Type 21 radar mattress fitted to the main director. *(US Navy)*

After modernisation, *Yamashiro*'s pagoda featured very heavy bracing on the rear and extended further aft than *Fuso*'s. *Fuso*'s No 3 turret was stowed facing forward after reconstruction. *Fuso* carried a catapult on the roof of No 3 turret from 1933 to 1941. *Yamashiro* only ever carried her aircraft on the quarterdeck. The forward-most pair of searchlights on *Fuso* was lower than the corresponding pair on *Yamashiro*.

Hyuga had an additional structure fitted to the front of the after funnel when the searchlight platforms were added in 1930 that was not fitted to *Ise*. After modernisation, the main topmast was fitted to the front of the mainmast on *Hyuga* and to the rear of the mainmast on *Ise*. *Ise* had an additional platform at the rear of the funnel searchlight tower that was not fitted to *Hyuga*. The pagoda bridge on *Hyuga* was open at the front on the third and fifth levels from the top; these had glazed screens on *Ise*. From May 1942 until her conversion in May 1943, *Hyuga* carried four triple 25mm in place of her No 5 turret.

Left: *Hyuga* in 1941 with degaussing cable in place and boat booms swung out. *(By courtesy of Ray Bean)*

***Fuso* 1933**
Fuso after her first modification. The 5in AA guns have been fitted and the quad 13mm mounts can be seen abreast the funnel and fore and aft of the bridge pagoda. The catapult is fitted to turret No 3 with the aircraft elevator and its rails alongside to port.

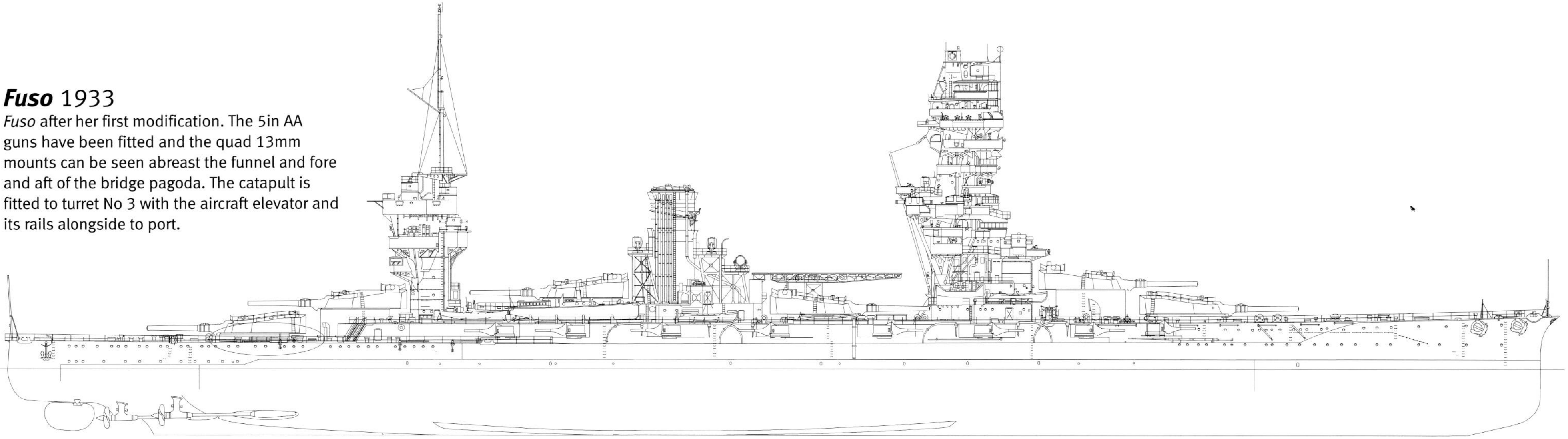

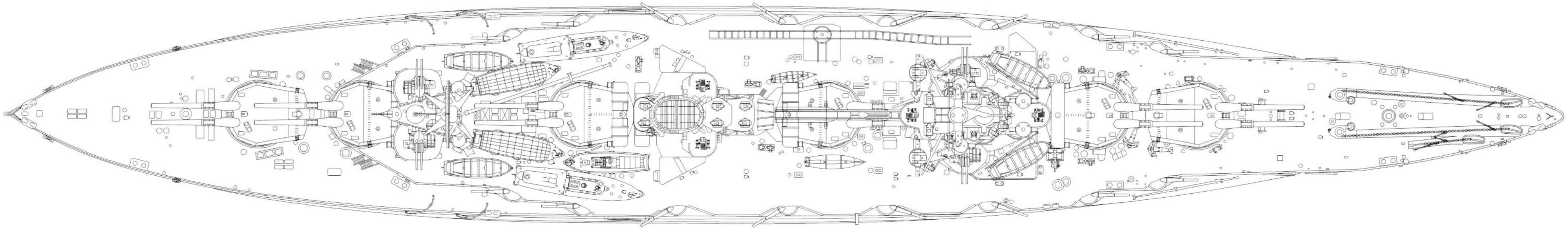

***Fuso* 1935**
Fuso after her second modification. The stern has been lengthened and the motor room for the crane fitted aft on the port side. The quad 13mm mounts still make up the light AA fit.

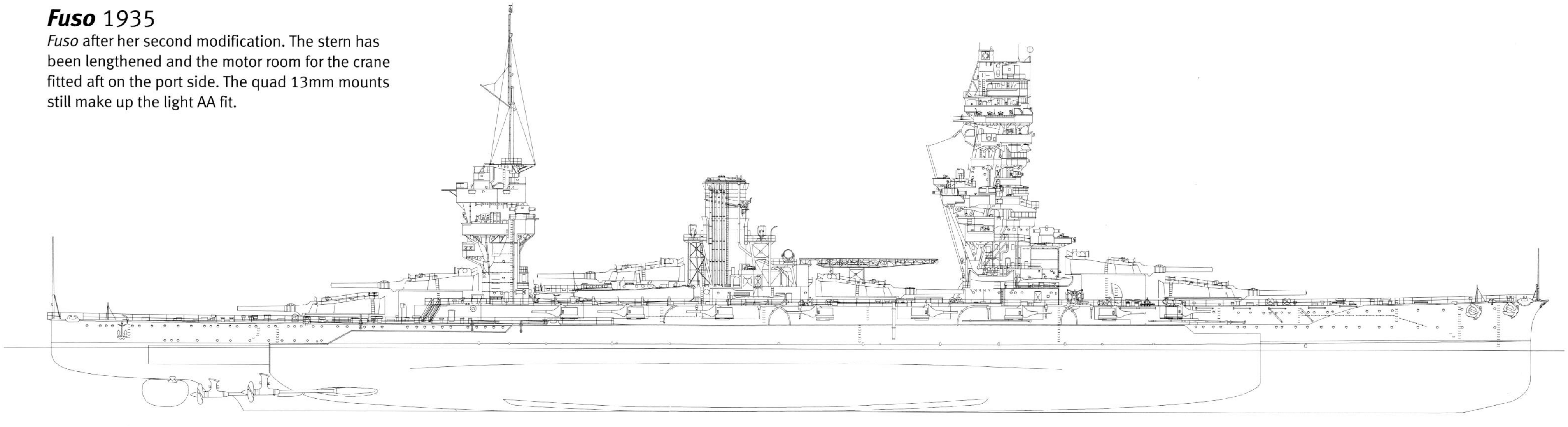

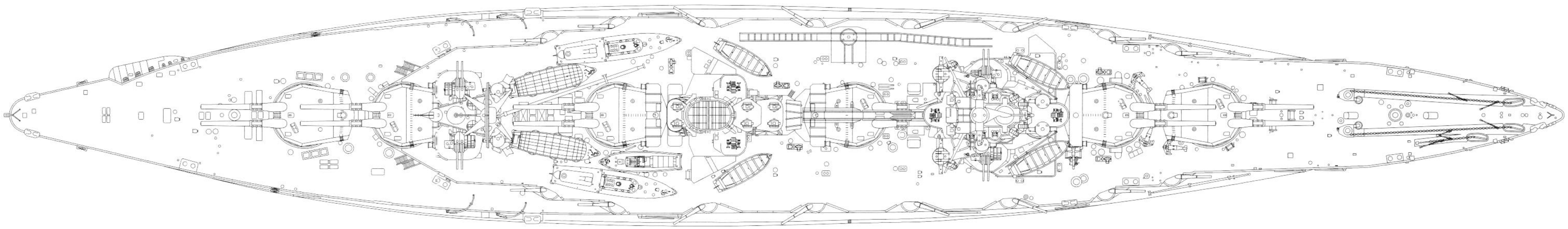

Fuso 1944

Fuso in her final guise, bristling with 25mm AA guns. The platform over the conning tower has been reduced in length due to the 25mm AA mounts fitted to the roof of turret No 2. The top of the bridge pagoda has been altered to incorporate the air defence position and a degaussing cable has been fitted. The extension port side aft has been enlarged to incorporate the aircraft crane when stowed. The aircraft deck does not continue under the barrels of turret No 6.

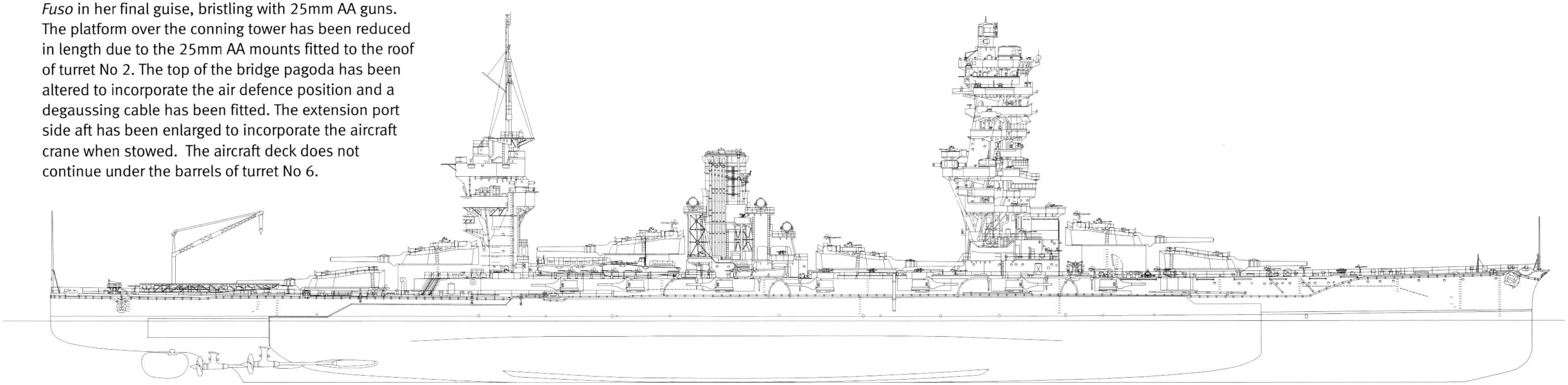

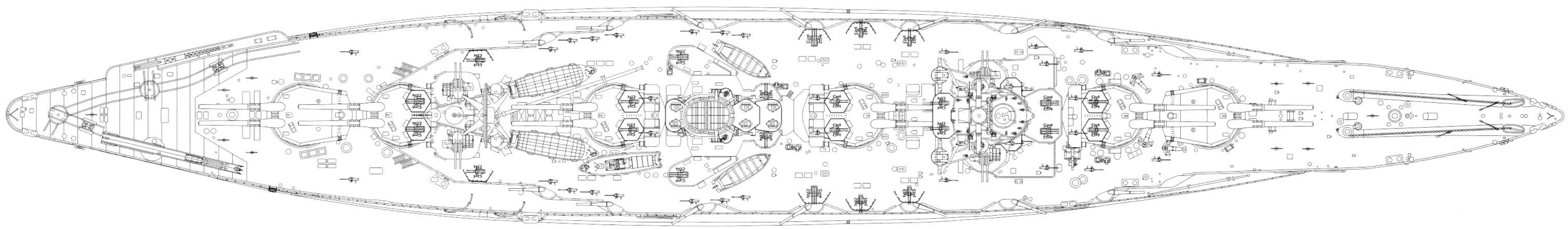

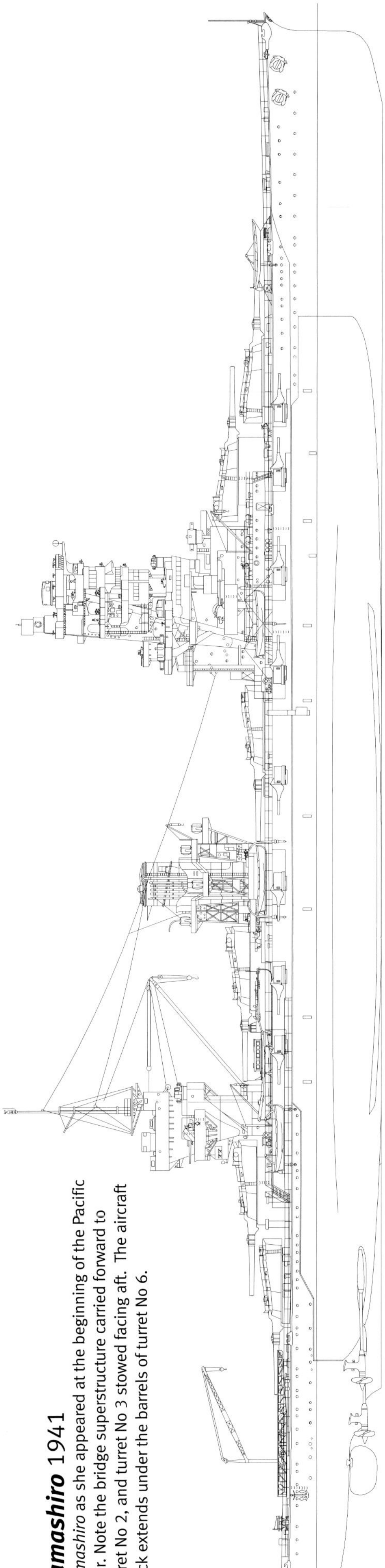

Yamashiro 1941
Yamashiro as she appeared at the beginning of the Pacific War. Note the bridge superstructure carried forward to turret No 2, and turret No 3 stowed facing aft. The aircraft deck extends under the barrels of turret No 6.

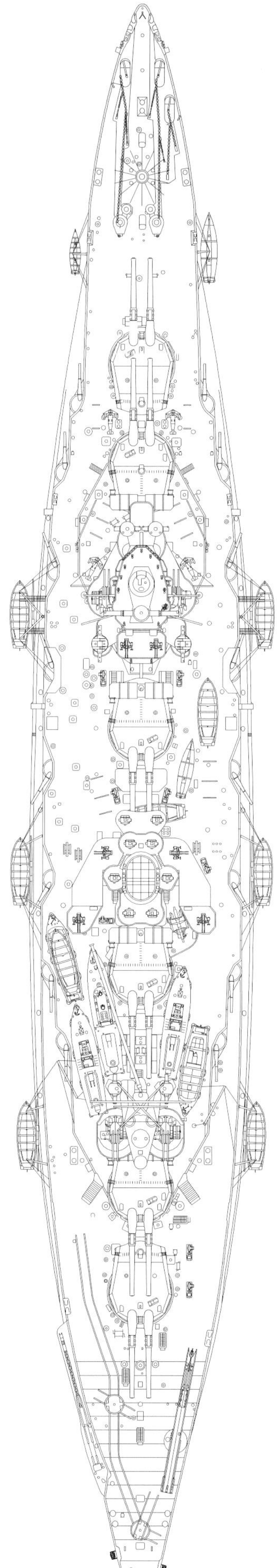

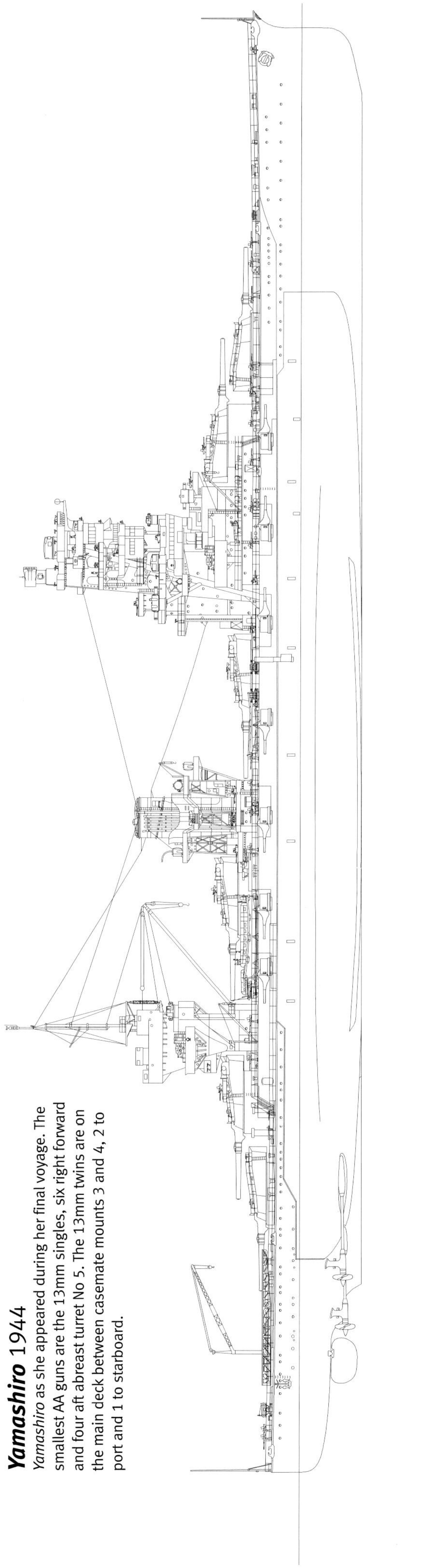

Yamashiro 1944
Yamashiro as she appeared during her final voyage. The smallest AA guns are the 13mm singles, six right forward and four aft abreast turret No 5. The 13mm twins are on the main deck between casemate mounts 3 and 4, 2 to port and 1 to starboard.

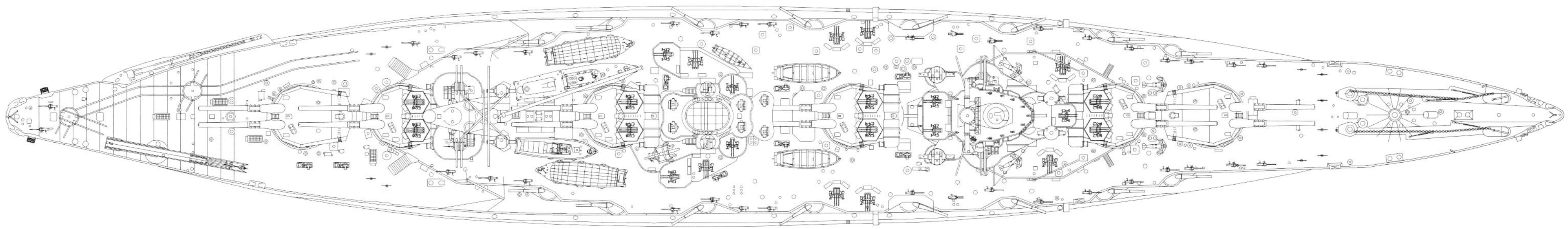

Hyuga 1941

Hyuga immediately prior to the war, unchanged since modernisation. The four twin 5in mounts are clustered around the foremast pagoda along with four twin 25mm mounts. An additional four twin 25mm are abreast the funnel, with the final pair aft of turret No 4.

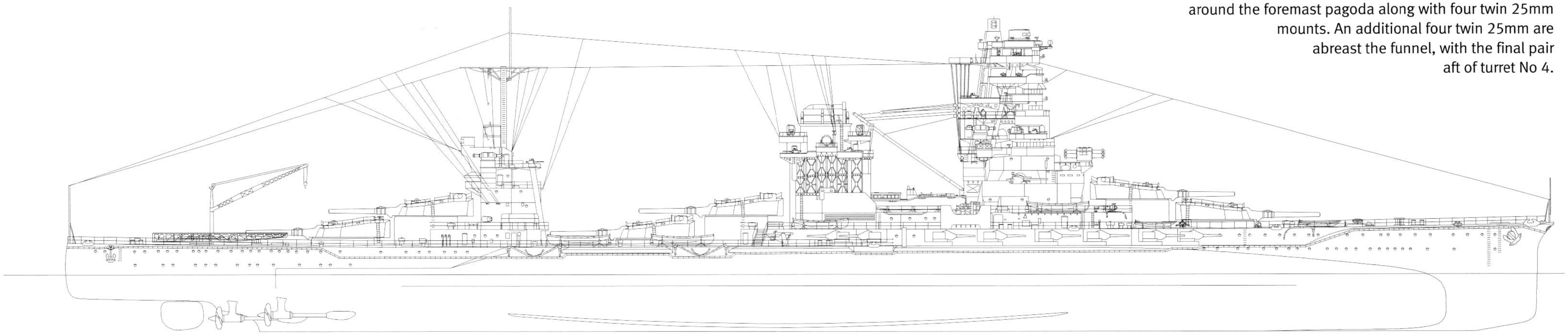

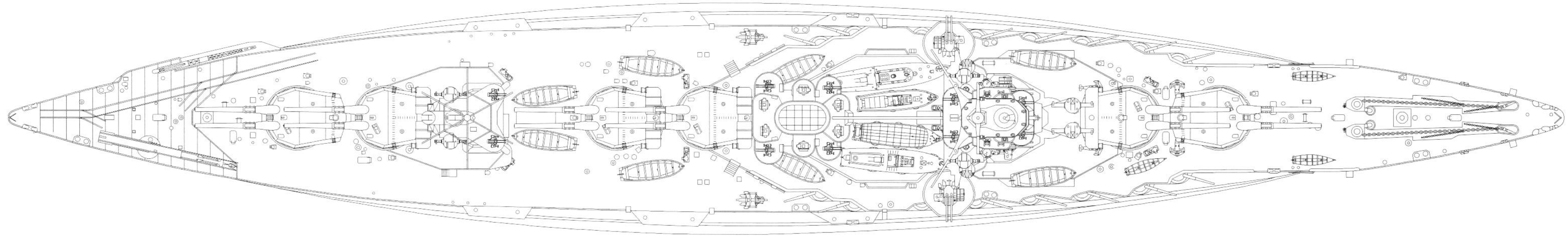

Hyuga 1942

Hyuga as she appeared after turret No 5 was replaced with four triple 25mm mounts.

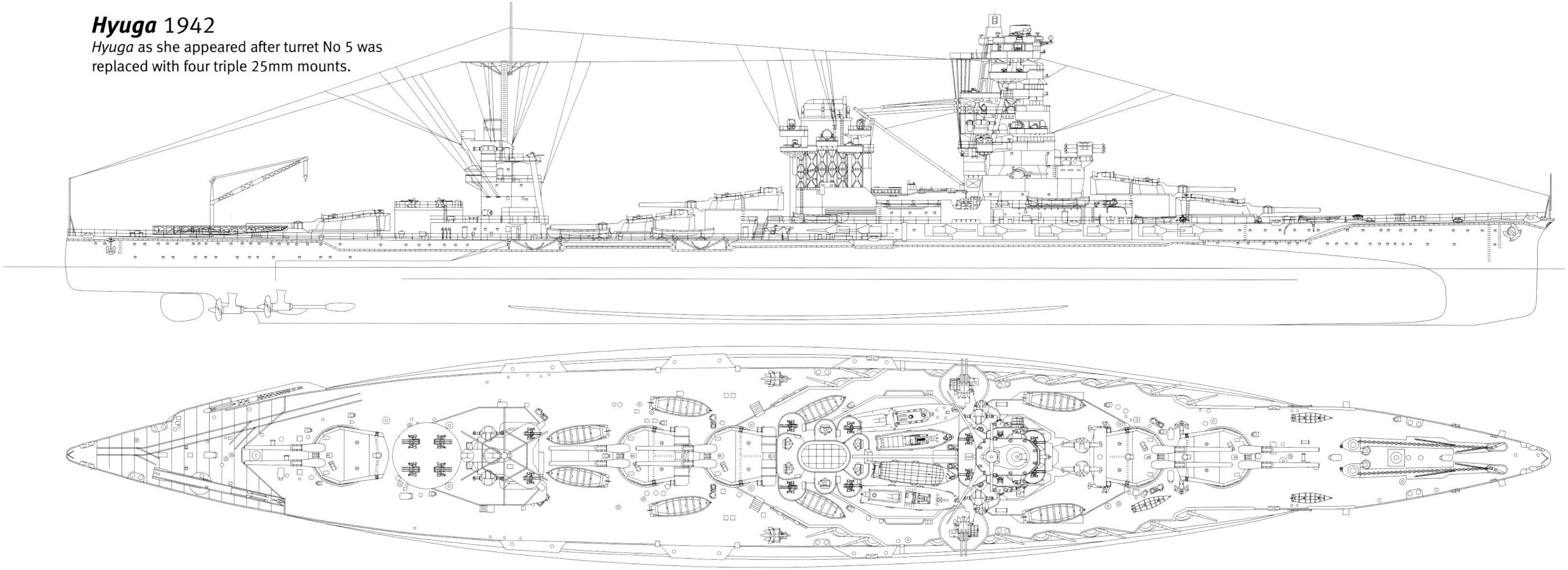

Ise 1944

Ise as she would have appeared at Cape Engaño with all AA upgrades fitted. Twenty-three of the thirty-one triple 25mm mounts are clearly visible, the remaining eight being on various levels and underneath overhangs on the bridge pagoda. Note the two landing barges abreast the funnel. The catapults were removed shortly after the battle in October 1944.

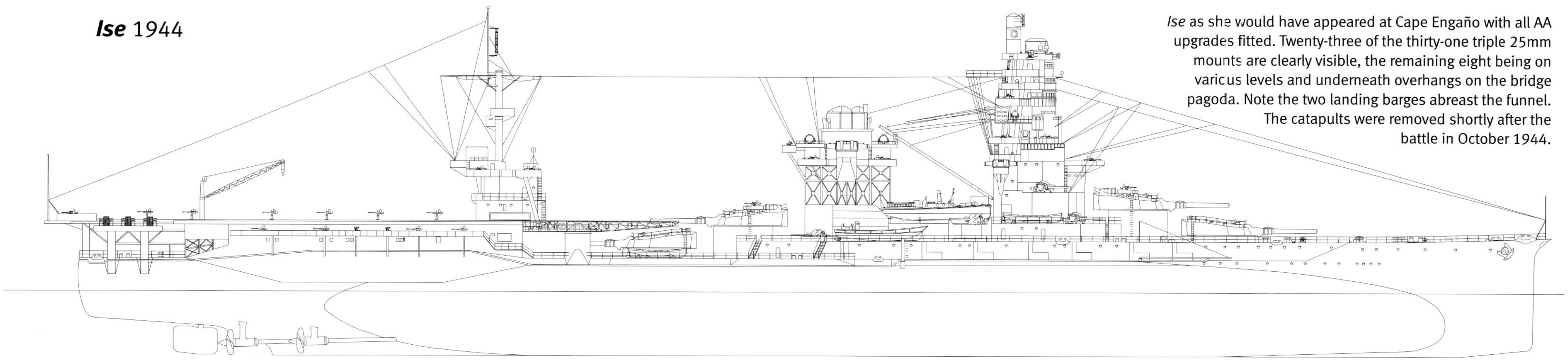

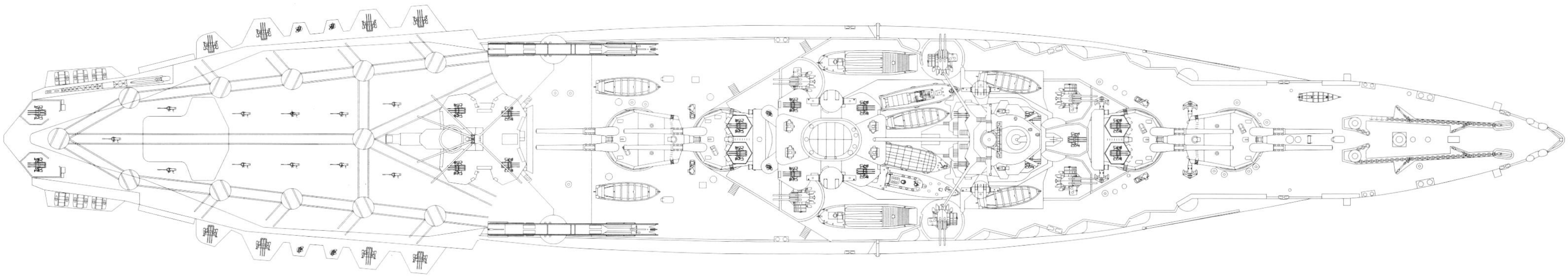

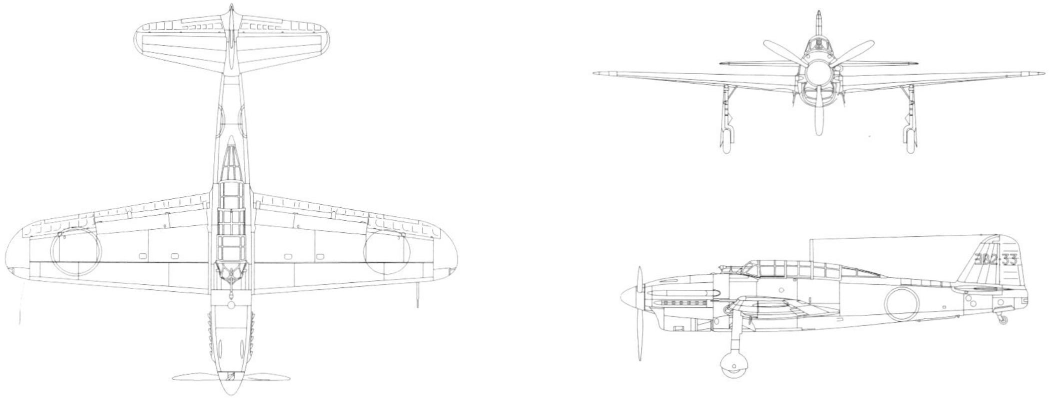

Yokosuka D4Y1 Suisei, code-named 'Judy'
Two-seat carrier-based dive-bomber, in service 1943–1945
Wingspan: 11.5m (37ft 9in)
Loaded weight: 3650kg (8047lbs)
Powerplant: One 12cyl liquid-cooled inverted vee engine;
max rating 1200hp for take-off
Max speed: 343mph @ 15,500ft
Normal range: 850nm
Bomb load: 310kg (683lbs)

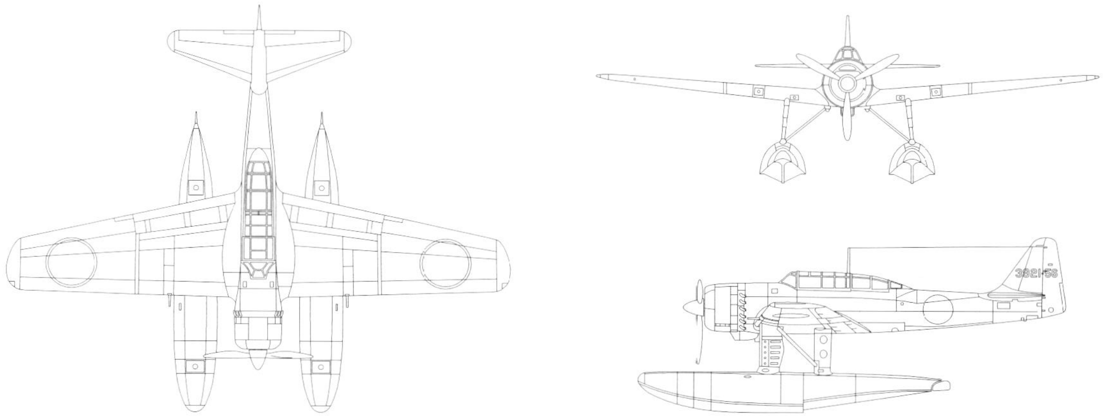

Aichi E16A1 Zuiun, code-named 'Paul'
Two-seat twin-float reconnaissance seaplane, in service 1944–1945
Wingspan: 12.81m (42ft 0in)
Loaded weight: 3900kg (8598lbs)
Powerplant: One 14cyl air-cooled radial engine;
max rating 1300hp for take-off
Max speed: 273mph @ 18,000ft
Normal range: 635nm
Bomb load: 250kg (551lbs)

Selected References

REFERENCES

Abe, Yasuo and Kishimoto, Sachio, *Maru Special #3 Fuso and Yamashiro,* (1975). Service history of *Fuso* and Yamashiro in photos and text. Japanese text.

Blair Jr, Clay, *Silent Victory* (J B Lippincott Company 1975). The very detailed story of US Submarine operations against Japan.

Brzeziński, Slawomir, *Profile Morksie 81: The Japanese Battleship Hyuga 1941* (Firma Wydawniczo-Handlowa 2006). Detailed appearance drawings of *Hyuga* in 1941 with accompanying photographs.

Burt, R A, *Japanese Battleships 1897-1945* (Seaforth Publishing 2015). A collection of photographs of all Japanese battleships that were ever placed in service. Arranged by class with technical details and informative captions, with many uncommon photos.

Dull, Paul S, *A Battle History of the Imperial Japanese Navy 1941-1945* (Naval Institute Press 1978). A very detailed account from the Japanese point of view of the battles fought by the IJN in the Pacific War.

Ito, Masanori, *The End of the Imperial Japanese Navy* (W W Norton 1984). A brief battle history of the IJN during WWII. The author knew many of the commanders and offers some interesting analyses.

Izumi, Kozo, *Japanese Battleships,* 2 Volumes (Grand Prix 2001). Very detailed technical reference of all the IJN battleships with many drawings and tables. Japanese text.

Jentschura, Hansgeorg; Jung, Dieter; Mickel, Peter, *Warships of the Imperial Japanese Navy, 1869-1945* (Arms & Armour Press 1977). Very detailed technical reference of all Imperial Japanese Navy warships with many data tables and drawings.

Lengerer, Hans and Rehm-Takahara, Tomoko, 'The 12cm Multiple Rocket Launcher of the Imperial Japanese Navy', *Warship IX* (Conway Maritime Press 1985). Article on the design, development, and deployment of the 12cm AA rocket system.

Lengerer, Hans, '*Ise* and *Hyuga*: The IJN's Hybrid Battleship-Carriers', *Warship 2009* (Conway Maritime Press 2009). A very detailed article on the conversion containing much background material.

Macintyre, Donald, *Leyte Gulf: Armada in the Pacific* (Ballantine Books 1970). A detailed account of the complex Battle of Leyte Gulf with many good maps.

Matsugi, Fujio, *Fuso Class Battleships – Gakken #30* (2001). A detailed technical history of *Fuso* and *Yamashiro.* Japanese text.

Skulski, Janusz, *Anatomy of the Ship: The Battleship Fuso* (Naval Institute Press, 1998). A very detailed technical reference of *Fuso*; packed with drawings and photographs.

Stille, Mark, *Imperial Japanese Navy Battleships 1941-45* (Osprey Publishing Ltd. 2008). A monograph on the twelve Japanese battleships that saw service in WWII; their background, weapons systems, alterations, and service histories.

Tully, Anthony P, *Battle of Surigao Strait* (Indiana University Press 2009). A very detailed account of the battle, interleaving US accounts with new primary Japanese source material; a well written story with plenty of fresh insights.

US Naval Intelligence, Japanese *Naval Vessels of World War Two* (Naval Institute Press 1987). A reprint of the ONI recognition handbook issued to US warships during WWII, focussing on recognition features of Japanese warships as seen from differing viewing angles.

Watts, Anthony J, *Japanese Warships of World War II* (Doubleday & Company, Inc. 1973). A comprehensive handbook with details of every Japanese vessel that served in World War II; many data tables, photos and line drawings.

Whitley, M J, *Battleships of World War Two – An International Encyclopedia* (Arms and Armour Press 1998). An extensive study of all the world's battleships that saw service in World War Two. Many photos and detailed service histories.

INTERNET REFERENCES

Fuso's Service History: http://www.combinedfleet.com/Fuso.htm

Hyuga's Service History: http://www.combinedfleet.com/Hyuga.htm

Ise's Service History: http://www.combinedfleet.com/Ise.htm

Yamashiro's Service History: http://www.combinedfleet.com/Yamashiro.htm

MODEL AND ACCESSORY MANUFACTURERS

www.aoshima-bk.co.jp/en/
www.artwox.com
www.digitalnavy.com/
www.flyhawkmodel.com/html/Flyhawkmodel/
www.goldmm.com/
www.lionroar.net/
www.konishimodel.sakura.ne.jp/english.htm
www.rainbowmodel.com/

SUPPLIERS OF SAMPLE KITS AND ACCESSORIES

abkmodels.com/
www.hobbyeasy.com/
www.imperialhobbies.ca/
www.stores.ebay.com/krakenhobbies

GENERAL INTEREST

www.modelshipwrights.com/
www.modelwarships.com/index1.html
www.combinedfleet.com/
www.steelnavy.net/